PAQ'BATLH: THE KLINGON EPIC. Copyright © 2022 by the authors, editors, and translator. This work carries a Creative Commons BY-NC-SA 4.0 International license, which means that you are free to copy and redistribute the material in any medium or format, and you may also remix, transform, and build upon the material, as long as you clearly attribute the work to the authors and editors (but not in a way that suggests the authors or punctum books endorses you and your work), you do not use this work for commercial gain in any form whatsoever, and that for any remixing and transformation, you distribute your rebuild under the same license. http://creativecommons.org/licenses/by-nc-sa/4.0/

First edition published in 2011 by Uitgeverij, Tirana/The Hague
Second edition published in 2022 by Uitgeverij
An imprint of punctum books, Earth, Milky Way
https://www.punctumbooks.com

ISBN-13: 978-1-68571-094-1 (print)
ISBN-13: 978-1-68571-095-8 (ePDF)
DOI: 10.53288/0345.1.00
LCCN: 2022939561
Library of Congress Cataloging Data is available from the Library of Congress

Book design: Vincent W.J. van Gerven Oei
Concept: Floris Schönfeld
Reconstruction: Kees Ligtelijn
Editing: Floris Schönfeld, Kees Ligtelijn, Vincent W.J. van Gerven Oei, and David Yonge-Mallo
Translation: Marc Okrand
Preface: DeSDu' jen puqloD

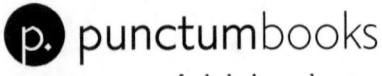

*spontaneous acts of scholarly combustion*

SCHÖNFELD ET AL. (EDS.)

# paq'batlh
# The Klingon Epic

TRANSLATED BY
MARC OKRAND

# Contents

Preface to the Second Edition – A Note on *no' Hol*     9
Introduction     21
Klingon Orthography and Pronunciation     39
Translator's Note     41

THE BOOK OF HONOR     48
  Prologue     50
  Ground Book     62
  Force Book     96
  Impact Book     172
  Epilogue     190

Bibliography     195

# paq 'ay'mey

| | |
|---|---|
| PAQ'BATLH | 49 |
| lut cherlu' | 51 |
| paq'yav | 63 |
| paq'raD | 97 |
| paq'QIH | 173 |
| bertlham | 191 |

The editors wish to dedicate this new version of the *paq'batlh* to HenraH Debvo' a.k.a. Henri van Zanten, Master of the Scream and surely one of the most Klingon Terrans we have known. May he continue his battles in Sto-vo-kor.

*qa' wIje'meH maSuv*
We fight to enrich the spirit

# Preface to the Second Edition
## A Note on *no' Hol*

In recent years, the Federation has taken significant measures to expand its database on the Klingon language and its numerous dialects. One of the greatest mysteries to date has been the classical version of the warrior's tongue, *no' Hol* (literally, "ancestors' language"). The study of the *paq'batlh*, as well as other works of ancient Klingon literature, was extremely uncommon among non-Klingons prior to the first edition of the Federation Standard translation published a decade ago. Similarly, study of the Empire's nonstandard tongues by outsiders is not typical. Knowledge regarding certain dialects of *tlhIngan Hol* was made known to citizens of the Federation only when Dr. Marc Okrand published his ground-breaking guide to quotidian Klingon language and customs, *Klingon for the Galactic Traveler*.[1]

---

[1] Marc Okrand, *Klingon for the Galactic Traveler* (New York: Pocket Books, 1997).

That too changed with the publication of the most recent translation of the *paq'batlh*, which included a romanized transcription from fragments of the Klingon creation myth — a tale still commonly told today in various versions during traditional Klingon weddings. The text, astonishingly, is presented in the original *no' Hol* with no translation into contemporary Klingon. Accompanying it is an English translation, rendering a deduction (or, at the very least, informed guesses) of key details regarding *no' Hol* possible. This text provides the most complete picture of ancient Klingon to date.

The role of *no' Hol* in Klingon society today is mainly a ceremonial one. Its phrases have been frozen in time by rituals such as the Rite of Ascension (*nentay*) and the Kot'baval festival (*Qotba'val*). Nonetheless, it still finds its way into everyday conversation through phrases that are so famous that they haven't changed for well over a thousand years. Aficionados of Klingon history, scholars, and members of the Klingon upper class might also hold conversations entirely in *no' Hol* as a symbol of stature or to show off their own knowledge of their people's history. This information could be particularly useful to diplomats and those seeking prized information regarding Qo'noS's past, which has remained somewhat a mystery. This information can, too, be useful for students of older forms of Klingon poetry. Those who are interested in reading such classics as the *paq'batlh*, any of G'trok's epic poems, or the libretti for the vast majority of Klingon operas in their original form will find a knowledge of *no' Hol* invaluable.

When one considers the religious and historical significance of *no' Hol*, it is easy to understand why details about it have remained a mystery for outsiders. The Klingons are a proud people, reverent towards their forebearers, and slow to trust non-Klingons with any information of import. Nonetheless, it was determined in the assembling of the second edition that a simplistic explanation of the differences between *ta' Hol* and its ancestor tongue would be beneficial for all. A special academic envoy has successfully delivered previously classified files directly from the home world's extensive databanks. The information these files provide are somewhat limited in scope, and yet, they have allowed us to confirm some of the deductions already made by some Terran scholars. It is our hope that this information will prove to be of interest for new students of the Klingon language and culture, as well as to seasoned academics. Due to lacunae in information we cannot call this a definitive guide nor one that can be deemed totally accurate. However, it should provide any student with the most basic understanding of the grammar of ancient Klingon.

We present this information with only the utmost respect and with the hope that it will deepen ties between the Klingon Empire and the diverse peoples of the United Federation of Planets.

## Word Order

In contemporary *ta' Hol*, the word order is generally OVS (that is, object-verb-subject). Barring toasts and other special situations, this is a fixed order. Consider:

*loD qIp yaS*
man hit officer
"The office hits the man."

Based off the *no' Hol* fragments we possess, as well as the information obtained from the homeworld's database, it is reasonable to surmise that this was not always the case. It appears that in *no' Hol*, the word order was instead OSV (that is, object–subject–verb):

*q'usru-tyeDi tlhengon viv*
power-their Klingon respect
"The Klingon respects their power."

## Suffixes

There are a number of suffixes in *no' Hol* which seem to have the same or similar functions as their *ta' Hol* descendants:

| *no' Hol* | *ta' Hol* | **English** |
| --- | --- | --- |
| -'ag' | -'egh | oneself |
| -bat/-ba' | -be' | not |
| -DoDi | -jaj | may |
| -Det | -DI' | when, as soon as |
| -Doq | -Daq | at, in, on (locative) |

| *-g'oty*  | *-ghach* | nominalizer       |
| *-lit*    | *-lu'*   | indefinite subject |
| *-loq'*   | *-laH*   | can               |
| *-muq'*   | *-moH*   | cause             |
| *-mut*    | *-mo'*   | because           |
| *-nesru*  | *-nIS*   | need              |
| *-qit*    | *-qu'*   | emphatic          |
| *-toq'*   | *-taH*   | continuous        |
| *-tyeDi*  | *-chaj*  | their             |
| *-tyiq*   | *-chuq*  | each other        |

Reading through the fragment titled *Dor* ("The End," literally "It Comes to a Close"), one might be surprised to see the phrase *teq 'qinmaa tyanmuq'*. The English translation present renders this phrase "They forged a heart"; however, it more literally means "The gods created/forged/formed a heart." What's so peculiar about this phrase is that the suffix *-maa*, presumed to be the ancestor of the *ta' Hol* plural suffix *-mey*, is used on the noun *'qin* "god." In *ta' Hol*, one would expect the suffix *-pu'*, the plural suffix for beings capable of speech. *-maa* is also used on *teq* "heart," whose modern equivalent *tIq* would normally take the plural suffix for body parts *-Du'*. This may well indicate that *-pu'* and *-Du'* came along only later in Klingon's development.

Another suffix which might not have existed in more ancient forms of the Klingon language is *-DIch*, used in modern Klingon to construct ordinal numbers. (e.g., *wa'DIch* "first," *wejmaHDIch* "thirtieth"). The word translated as "second" in one of the fragments we possess is simply *tyot*, which may simply be the word for two. This word follows the noun it modifies (*teq*). In modern Klingon, such a construct is still possible, though the meaning is slightly different. Consider these phrases in *ta' Hol*:

*tIq cha'*       "heart #2"
*tIq cha'DIch*   "the second heart"

Alternatively, though, *tyot* could prove to be a word in its own right meaning "second" all the time, separate from the word *tyo* "two" found elsewhere in the *no' Hol* fragments. Yet another possibility is that these are two forms of the same word and that the terminal -*t* is an ancient suffix whose meaning is close to or the same as the modern -*DIch*.

## Prefixes

Modern Klingon uses a complex system of verb prefixes to communicate the subject and object of any given action. It would seem that these prefixes too have changed somewhat over the centuries. While we cannot determine whether any new prefixes have been introduced to the language based off our limited knowledge, we can determine that some older prefixes have disappeared. These are:

*me-*   "they–them"
*'u-*    "they–none"

Both of these prefixes have been replaced by the null prefix in *ta' Hol*. That is, these subject-object pairs are represented by no prefix in particular.

## Sound Shifts

It should come as no surprise that the sounds of Klingon have changed since the days of Kahless. These changes can be tracked by comparing ancient vocabulary with the known Klingon lexicon. Based off this deductive process, we can come to a loose understanding of how vowels and consonants have shifted over time.[2] Note that what is presented here is by no means definitive or the rule for how sounds changed in all words. Rather, these are general tendencies which have been remarked.

**Vowels**

| *no' Hol* | *ta' Hol* |
|---|---|
| a | a |
| aa | ey |
| e | a or I |
| o | a |
| oo | aw |
| u | o or u |

---

[2] See *Klingon Wiki*, s.v. "paq'batlh ancient Klingon," http://klingon.wiki/En/PaqbatlhAncientKlingon.

## Consonants

| no' Hol | ta' Hol |
|---------|---------|
| ty | ch |
| Di | j |
| Dy | j |
| g' | gh |
| q' | H |
| 'q | Q |
| s | S |
| sr | S |
| sy | S |
| t | final ' |

## Known Vocabulary in Ancient Klingon

| no' Hol | ta' Hol | English |
|---------|---------|---------|
| at | 'ej | and (conj.) |
| beng | bIng | below, area below (n.) |
| bosru | baS | metal (n.) |
| Doq | Daq | place (n.) |

| | | |
|---|---|---|
| Doq' | DaH | now (adv.) |
| Dur | Dor | end (v.) |
| Dya | je | and (conj.) |
| Dyav | jev | storm (v.) |
| 'eDi | 'Ij | listen (v.) |
| 'eDyay | jey | defeat (v.) |
| 'ew | 'Iw | blood (n.) |
| g'ir | ghur | increase (v.) |
| g'ub | ghob | fight, battle, do battle (v.) |
| jotlh | jatlh | speak (v.) |
| juq | joq | flutter, beat (heart) (v.) |
| lil | lul | fight (v.) |
| lub | lob | obey (v.) |
| moy' | may' | battle (n.) |
| mu'qberet | moQbara' | mok'bara (n.) |
| netabq'ot | nItebHa' | together, combined (adv.) |
| nev | nIv | be superior (v.) |
| pog' | pagh | nothing, nobody, zero (n.) |
| pung | pong | name (v.) |
| qil | qul | fire (n.) |
| qit | qu' | be fierce (v.) |

| | | |
|---|---|---|
| qoD | qaD | challenge (v.) |
| qom | qam | foot (n.) |
| 'qoot | Qaw' | destroy (v.) |
| quq' | qoH | fool (n.) |
| q'op | Hap | matter (n.) |
| q'usru | HoS | power (n.) |
| q'uty | Hoch | everything (n.) |
| 'qin | Qun | god (n.) |
| 'qi'tu' | QI'tu' | Paradise (n.) |
| srib | Sub | be solid (v.) |
| srim | Sum | be close (v.) |
| sye'q | SIQ | endure, bear (v.) |
| syisi | SuS | wind (n.) |
| teq | tIq | heart (n.) |
| tlhengon | tlhIngan | Klingon (n.) |
| tlhip | tlhup | whisper (v.) |
| tog' | tagh | begin (v.) |
| tub | tob | prove, test conclusively (v.) |
| tunsroot | tonSaw' | fighting technique |
| tyan | chen | take form (v.) |
| tyanmuq' | chenmoH | make, forge (v.) |

| | | |
|---|---|---|
| *tyo* | *cha'* | two (num.) |
| *tyot* | *cha'DIch* | second (num.) |
| *'ach* | *'ach* | but (conj.) |
| *'uq'* | *'oH* | it (pro.) |
| *viv* | *vuv* | respect (v.) |
| *wob* | *wab* | sound (n.) |

—DeSDu' jen puqloD

# Introduction

It is the aim of this publication to reconstruct the Klingon (*tlhIngan*)[1] epic of the *paq'batlh* for a Terran audience for the first time. Although the existence of a manuscript entitled *paq'batlh* has been known to us on Earth for some time, a comprehensive study of this great epic has so far not been attempted.

We acknowledge that many original sources of the text are still to be uncovered, and that what we present here is but a beginning in the study of this great Klingon cultural artifact. However, we hope that our efforts may offer a much-needed introduction to a fascinating epic and that this will lead to a more in-depth research of Klingon literature. In doing so we hope to have honored the well-worn Klingon proverb "We fight to enrich the spirit" (*qa' wIje'meH maSuv*).

---

[1] Klingon translations between parentheses follow the official transliteration of the Klingon language in the Roman alphabet, as first proposed by Marc Okrand, *The Klingon Dictionary* (New York: Pocket Books, 1992), 13-16.

## KAHLESS THE UNFORGETTABLE:
## LEGENDARY AND HISTORICAL FIGURE.

The *paq'batlh*, or *Book of Honor*, from "book" (*paq*) and "honor" (*batlh*), is a tale of epic proportions that is comparable to the Terran adventures of Hercules, Ulysses, Aeneas, or Gilgameš. And like these great cultural narratives, the *paq'batlh* too has a hero figure at its center, Kahless (*qeylIS*) the Unforgettable. The figure of Kahless has had a profound impact on Klingon culture. His teachings of honor and tradition form the basis of modern Klingon philosophy and culture. Kahless is still worshiped as a semi-divine figure by the Klingons of today. The stories of Kahless are known across the Klingon Empire, passed down from generation to generation, reminding the Klingon people of what they are and whence they came.

In Klingon culture Kahless figures both in a legendary and historical context, and these two personas tend to merge in the manner in which he is approached in Klingon texts. Kahless the legendary figure is possibly the more prolific of the two. As such he has taken on a semi-divine status incomparable to any other figure in Klingon culture. The Klingons stopped worshiping supernatural deities at some point in their history.[2] By doing so the Klingons took responsibility for their own existence and rid themselves of any external authoritative power.

There is a general misunderstanding surrounding the *paq'batlh* as being a type of Klingon Bible or Qur'an, containing a coherent set of rules by which one ought to abide.

---

[2] This is recounted in the creation myth in which the gods are destroyed by the combined strength of Klingon hearts they created; see *Prologue* 1.

However, the *paq'batlh* as transmitted through its textual tradition is a collection of stories recounting the life and deeds of Kahless the Unforgettable without any supplementary analysis or formulation of a clear code of conduct. The deeds of Kahless provide a level of moral guidance for Klingon society without being explicitly moralistic. Every Klingon should draw his or her own conclusions from Kahless's deeds, and carries the responsibility of finding a personal way of applying these conclusions to his or her own existence. So Kahless the legend has a sustained, almost personalized role in Klingon culture, guiding warriors through life to the gates of the Klingon Valhalla, Sto-vo-kor (*Suto'vo'qor*), which he guards.[3]

Kahless the historical figure is considered to be the first Warrior King and Emperor of the Klingon Empire, after defeating his enemies some time in the 9th century (Terran calendar). His name is commonly accompanied by the epithet "The Unforgettable" (*lIjlaHbogh pagh*[4]) or "The Greatest Warrior of Them All" (*SuvwI' Dun law' Hoch Dun puS*). Neither his date of birth nor his provenance are well known. There have been a number of attempts to track down information about the historical figure Kahless on Earth by, among others, Michael-Jan Friedman in his book *Kahless*.[5] However, such reconstructions based on historical evidence diverge at several significant points from the

---

3   See *paq'QIH* 5.
4   Both *qeylIS lIjlaHbogh pagh* and *qeylIS'e' lIjlaHbe'bogh vay'* are correct. The version in the *paq'batlh* is older. Traditionally, the phrase *lIjlaHbogh pagh* is applied to Kahless only, while the newer *lIjlaHbe'bogh vay'* may be applied to Kahless and other leaders/heroes as well. It would be a sign of extreme arrogance or disrespect to use the *lIjlaHbogh pagh* version for anyone other than Kahless."
5   Michael-Jan Friedman, *Kahless* (New York: Pocket Books, 1997).

version as reconstructed in this book, which solely relies on textual evidence. We have thus decided to leave the historical figure of Kahless to the historians and archeologists, for it is the myth, not the historical figure who continues to capture the imagination of countless generations of Klingons.

## SYNOPSIS OF THE *PAQ'BATLH*

The *paq'batlh* consists of a prologue (*lut cherlu'*), the main body of text that is broken into three parts, the "Ground" (*yav*), "Force" (*raD*), and "Impact" (*QIH*) books (*paq*), and an epilogue (*bertlham*).

The prologue, which in this publication has been included as several *no' Hol* fragments (see below) recounts the Klingon creation myth in which the gods created the first Klingon hearts. Once those two hearts started beating together they created such a powerful sound that they destroyed the gods and everything created before them. After the prologue, the narrative of Kahless commences.

The first book is called "Ground Book" (*paq'yav*). Kahless and his younger brother Morath (*moratlh*) are out hunting *targ*.[6] Morath throws his spear too soon and fails to kill the prey, leaving him behind with a wounded pride. Molor, the reigning tyrant of the Klingon empire, witnesses the scene and approaches Morath as soon as Kahless has gone. He offers Morath a chance to become leader of his House if he succeeds in persuading his father to surrender to him. Morath decides to betray his family. Late that night

---

6 See *paq'yav* 1, note ad loc.

Morath goes to his father to claim the family sword, which, however, his father refuses to hand over. Morath tries to take it from him but his father resists. Eventually, the father is mortally wounded by Morath, who runs away with the sword. Meanwhile Kahless enters the chamber only to find his father dying.

Promising to avenge his family honor, Kahless storms off in pursuit of Morath. Kahless chases his younger brother until they arrive at the foot of the Kri'stak (*QIStaq*) volcano. Here they fight for twelve days and twelve nights until Morath throws himself in the volcano, taking the family sword with him.[7]

While Kahless laments his fate at the top of the volcano, he is overheard by an old warrior who encourages him to look for his brother and father in Gre'thor (*ghe'tor*), the Klingon Underworld. Kahless descends into the mouth of the volcano and using his own hair he crafts a fine sword from the magma, the first *bat'leth* (*betleH*). Kahless takes the sword with him as he enters the Underworld through the volcano.

In the "Force Book" (*paq'raD*) Kahless enters Gre'thor. In order to pass the gates of the realm of the dead unnoticed, Kahless must trick the gatekeeper, the fearsome Fek'lhr (*veqlargh*). He does so by blinding the gatekeeper with a ray of light reflecting off his sword. Once inside the Underworld, he encounters his father and brother. He offers Morath forgiveness if he comes with him back to the world of the living and joins him in his fight with the tyrant Molor. Morath swears allegiance to Kahless who subsequently shows his brother and father the forms of the mok'bara

---

[7] In some versions of the story, Morath throws the sword into the sea. See TNG:6x17.

(*moQbara'*)[8] through which they are able to reenter their bodies and return to the land of the living.

Kortar (*qortar*),[9] the ruler of the Underworld, notices that two of his souls are missing. He flies into a rage and calls upon the Qempa'keh (*qempa'QeH*, the Warriors of the Dead) to join him in retrieving the souls of Morath and his father and bringing Kahless to justice.

Kahless, his brother, and their father travel the Klingon kingdoms to amass support for their fight against Molor. Kahless arrives at the city of Qam-Chee (*qamchIy*) and recounts his adventures to the inhabitants. Meanwhile, a party of Molor's soldiers knocks at the gates demanding they hand over the fugitive. Kahless asks the people of Qam-Chee for assistance in fighting Molor's men. All but a young woman by the name of Lukara (*luqara'*) refuse. Together Kahless and Lukara fight against Molor's men and after defeating them make love in the blood of their enemies. Kahless and Lukara join the other rebel forces at the river Skral (*SIqral*). Here Kahless gives a speech calling upon his troops to be victorious over the forces of Molor.

Kortar and the Qempa'keh, having seen the damage that Kahless caused at Qam-chee, confront Kahless with his theft of the souls of his brother and father. Kahless explains his intentions and, realizing they are honorable, Kortar decides to join forces with Kahless in his fight against Molor. Kahless makes Kortar promise that from then on honorable warriors go to a specific part of the Underworld where they can do honorable battle for all eternity. Thus Kortar promises to create Sto-vo-kor.

---

[8] See *paq'raD* 3, note ad loc.
[9] Sometimes transcribed "Kotar."

The armies of Molor and Kahless meet at the three forks of the river Skral and wage war. Morath and his father are slain in battle, finally achieving an honorable death. Kahless shouts out to Kortar to keep his promise to grant them passage to Sto-vo-kor.

Kahless finds Molor on the battlefield, and after a brief exchange of challenges they fight. Finally, after a long, hard battle, the victorious Kahless cuts out Molor's hearts, and in doing so restores Molor's honor as the tyrant died an honorable death in combat. Kahless then washes the hearts in the river Skral, releasing Molor.[10]

The "Impact Book" (*paq'QIH*) opens with Kahless's unification of the Klingon tribes and his becoming the first Emperor of the Klingon Empire. He teaches the Klingons the ways of honor and thus creates the foundation of Klingon culture. One day he decides that it is time to rejoin his family in the Underworld and, going to the edge of the city, he bids farewell to his people. In his final speech he reminds the Klingons that they must always rely on no one but themselves. Lukara helps Kahless commit ritual suicide (*Heghbat*) so he can join his father and brother in the Underworld. She too screams up to Kortar that a great warrior is coming and in her scream she is joined by the whole Klingon race.

Kahless meets Kortar at the border of Gre'thor where he tells him that he has kept his promise to divide the Underworld in two parts. One is called Sto-vo-kor, the realm of the honorable where warriors do eternal battle and celebrate their honor, and the other one is called Gre'thor, where the dishonored end up, guarded by Kortar and his

---

10 See *paq'yav* 4, note ad loc.

Fek'lhr. Having arrived at Sto-vo-kor, Kahless is given a hero's welcome and Kortar entrusts him with the task of guarding the realm, allowing only honorable warriors to enter.

The epilogue summarizes the moral content of the *paq'yav, paq'raD,* and *paq'QIH* for the listener. It reminds all Klingons to remember the stories of Kahless, to pass them on to their children so that they will remain unforgettable for ever.

## RECONSTRUCTION OF THE *PAQ'BATLH*

The origin of the *paq'batlh* in its current form is not known to scholars on Earth. We know that the stories of Kahless were collected and originally written down in the "ancestors' language" (*no' Hol*), which is currently still in use throughout the Klingon Empire within specific religious and historical contexts. However, the study of *no' Hol* is a privilege that is only granted to a very select group of Klingon scholars and religious leaders and is discouraged among non-Klingons. Whereas the details concerning this ancient language are elaborated by Marc Okrand in his translator's note and by DeSDu' in the Preface, we would like to stress that it is only with the utmost respect and reverence that we have included these fragments. We are nevertheless very excited to be able to include a fragment of the original *no' Hol* prologue to the *paq'batlh* (henceforth, OP) in this publication. As far as we are aware, this is the first fragment of *no' Hol* to be published by a Terran publishing house.

The prologue tells the origin myth of the Klingons in three parts: the first Klingon hearts, the creation of the first Klingons, and the origin of their home planet Kronos (*Qo'noS*). This section of the epic is definitely one of the most ancient elements in Klingon mythology. According to our current knowledge of the development of Klingon culture and language, the op fragments can be dated at about 500 QBN (*qeylIS bov nubwI'*, "before the era of Kahless").[11] The fragments were part of the estate of an anonymous collector who donated them to the Museum Volkenkunde in Leiden, the Netherlands. We are very grateful to the museum for allowing autoptic examination of the fragments. Due to the fact that the fragments were written on very perishable materials, such as untreated animal hides[12] as was customary at the time, only a small part of what we believe to be a significantly larger body of text has survived the passage of time. Even though they are among the oldest Klingon artifacts to have ever been found on Earth, their style, written in the third person and obeying a 3-6 line verse structure already reveals the dominant form of classical Klingon tripartite compositional structure.

As for the reconstruction of the epic's main textual body, it has not been our intention to reconstruct an "original" version of the *paq'batlh,* based on ancient sources only. First of all it has been our aim to provide the reader, both Klingon and Terran, with a version of the story that is as complete as possible, while recreating what we be-

---

11  About 3rd-4th century CE. Dates are stated in terms of QBN (*qeylIS bov nubwI'*, "before the era of Kahless") or QB (*qeylIS bov,* "the era of Kahless"). Unfortunately, the Klingon time measuring and dating system has as of yet not received the academic study it deserves.
12  Possibly *targ* hides, see *paq'yav* 2, note ad loc.

lieve is a natural stylistic balance in the work that would somewhat resemble other Klingon literary material of the period in which the *paq'batlh* saw its first flourishing as classical epic. In this effort we have also been guided by earlier philological projects such as Nick Nicholas and Andrew Strader's reconstruction of the tragedy of *Hamlet*.[13]

In our reconstruction of the "original" text, the translation process has proceeded in both directions, meaning both from Klingon to English and from English to Klingon. This way working was necessitated by the material at our disposal, which comprised both English and Klingon sources. The textual material was reconstructed and collated by Kees Ligtelijn and subsequently edited to a "complete" version by Floris Schönfeld, artistic director of the Klingon-Terran Research Ensemble (KTRE). The large majority of the translations was produced by Klingon language expert Marc Okrand, assisted by the scholars from the Klingon Language Institute and Klingon speakers during two Klingon *qep'a'mey*, or "large meetings."[14] We hereby wish to express our gratitude for the enormous work they have accomplished.

The version of *paq'batlh* that we decided largely to adhere to is based on the only English translation available outside adaptations in traditional Klingon opera,[15] namely

---

13 William Shakespeare, *Hamlet, Prince of Denmark*, rest. Nick Nicholas and Andrew Strader (New York: Pocket Books, 2000).
14 For a detailed account of a *qep'a'* meeting, we refer to Arika Okrent, *In The Land of Invented Languages: Adventures in Linguistic Creativity, Madness, and Genius* (New York: Spiegel & Grau, 2009), 273-78.
15 Klingons are adamant lovers of opera, which, however, differs in many respects from the Terran opera tradition. For example, the audience is often involved by chanting along parts of the libretto, actors may play multiple roles, and putting the character masks on and off is an integral part of the dramatic action.

the so-called Standard Version (henceforth, SV). SV comprises a number of corrupted digital files recovered from a server of the University of Heidelberg, containing large portions of the *paq'batlh* text. Although the translator remains unknown, an ex-researcher from the department of astronomy has confirmed to us that the files may have belonged to a scientist once working on the SETI project. However, neither SETI nor the University of Heidelberg have been able to confirm the existence of the researcher in question.

Moreover, due to a damaged file header, neither production date, authorship, provenance, nor chronology can be established. Our reason for nonetheless using this material is its striking similarity to other extant sources, in particular the libretto reconstructed for the Klingon opera *'u'* (henceforth, O), which was written in modern Klingon, covering scenes from the *paq'yav, paq'raD, paq'QIH,* and epilogue. We believe that the researcher in question was working on a translation of the *paq'batlh* from either the *no' Hol* or modern Klingon version before the project was aborted for unknown reasons. After careful deliberation with translator Marc Okrand we decided to retranslate the SV material back into modern Klingon, supplemented with material from other available Klingon sources.

SV is written in the third person and follows a three-line verse structure characteristic of the classical period of Klingon literature. This style is referred to as "narrator style" (*Qich'lut*), and in this version rendered as spoken by the so-called Master of the Scream (*jachwI'na'*, "true screamer"), the traditional narrator role in Klingon opera.

Another set of sources comprises written documents in various stages of the Klingon language, from *no' Hol* to the modern standard language. We know that the stories of Kahless almost certainly had a rich oral history before they were eventually written down. As Klingon culture had and still has a very lively oral tradition of storytelling, it would be reasonable to expect that the creation of the epic was based on a number of orally transmitted stories dating back a number of centuries before they were written down.

Evidence for this theory may be found in the fact that a number of known Kahless stories is not included in the *paq'batlh* but can nonetheless be traced in the text. Well known is the story, not collected in the *paq'batlh*, of a storm approaching the city of Quin'lat.

> Everyone took protection within the city walls except one man who remained outside. Kahless went to him and asked what he was doing. "I am not afraid," the man said. "I will not hide my face behind stone and mortar. I will stand before the wind and make it respect me." Kahless honored his choice and went back inside. The next day, the storm came, and the man was killed. Kahless reacted with the famous line, "The wind does not respect a fool" (*qoH vuvbe' SuS*).[16]

The conclusion of this story is echoed on the *no' Hol* prologue to the *paq'batlh*.[17] This divergence in textual material suggests that there were numerous versions of the stories in circulation at the time the *paq'batlh* version known to us was compiled.

---

16 See TNG:6x23.
17 See *Prologue* 2.9: *quq' syisi vivbat*.

The assumption that the *paq'batlh* is based on an oral tradition is further supported by the fact that many passages from the Kahless epic have survived in the tradition of Klingon battle opera (*may' ghe'naQ*), which is deeply ingrained in Klingon culture. According to certain sources, the form of Klingon opera we know goes back to the pre-Kahless period (c. 900 CE). We can assume the narrative devices and musical arrangements have since become more complex, yet the general *may' ghe'naQ* form still seems to be linked directly to the pre-Kahless form.

Traditional Klingon opera (*ghe'naQ nIt*) has a well-established form[18] that has changed little over the last millennium. The form seems to have survived due to its integration into religious and secular ceremonies; operas with a mythological or military theme are often related to public festivals or celebrations.

The main operatic work in the Klingon cultural tradition which has retained a large portion of the story line of the Kahless epic is called *'u'*. This opera, as well as other works that feature the stories of Kahless, are most often performed during the Kot'baval festival[19] which celebrates the life and deeds of this Klingon hero, especially his defeat of the tyrant Molor.[20]

A contemporary Klingon audience will be able to "read" the opera being performed with great subtlety, partially because of the consistency in form. To an audience not

---

18 The manuscript known as the *Book of the Perfect Scream* (*paq'jachchu*) is a main source in reconstructing classic Klingon opera, as it contains musicological wisdoms and techniques. Its standard version can be dated at around 550 QB.
19 See *Memory Alpha*, s.v. "Kot'baval Festival," https://memory-alpha.fandom.com/wiki/Kot%27baval_Festival.
20 See *paq'raD* 23.

familiar with the ways of Klingon opera, it may seem at times somewhat abstract, only to suddenly become highly volatile in its theatrical power. This is in part caused by the fact that only a few scenes from a larger story line are shown, which everyone is familiar with. Whereas a Klingon audience has no problems filling in the gaps, a Terran audience may be surprised by the great leaps, both in time and in space, which are in full violation of the unity of time and space classically imposed by the Aristotelean tragic framework.

The earliest material evidence we have of the opera *'u'* can be traced back to the so-called Kijkduin Stones (henceforth, TL). These three triangular stones bearing carvings of supposedly *no' Hol* fragments and pictographs, which are thought to be used as a musical score, contain fragments of two scenes from *paq'raD,* namely those of the battle between Kahless and his brother Morath, the love scene between Kahless and Lukara, and the short story of "The Fool and the Wind" (*qoH SuS je*), recounting the story mentioned above, in which Kahless visits the city of Quin'lat during a fierce storm. The style of the pictographs and inscription suggests that the stones date from 100–150 QB. The three-sided rectangular stones are said to be found near the beach of Kijkduin, a neighborhood of The Hague, the Netherlands. We were able to access the stones for autoptic examination in the storage of the Interfaculty ArtScience in The Hague, where they are currently kept.

*'u'* was given its Terran premiere by the KTRE under the artistic direction of Schönfeld, taking place in September 2010 in the Zeebelt Theater in The Hague. As said, the similarities between O and SV are striking and have to a large

extent facilitated the reverse translation of sv to the original Klingon.

The main difference between these two sources is that sv is written in the third person, whereas o is mainly narrated from the first person perspective in the so-called "aria style" (*Huy'reH*).

These were complemented with the aforementioned *Qich'lut* parts, in which a narrator recounts part of the story line and actively engages the audience. It seems logical that the first person parts of o, in which the protagonists relate the story from their own point of view, were adapted from the original Klingon version of sv, in order to be suitable for stage performance with multiple actors. This would suggest a development from poetic monologue to the current polyphonic opera form. It remains unclear whether the function of the chorus, which in modern Klingon opera comprises all the actors, can already be distinguished in sv. Schönfeld's research however has shown that there are distinctive parts in sv with a common style, here referred to with "chorus style" (*cha'ang*), often containing moralizing elements and addressing one or more actors directly. Owing to the difficulty of determining the exact differentiation between the role of the Master of the Scream and the chorus, both have been conflated into the Master's function.

## THE TRADITION OF KLINGON OPERA

The Klingons have very distinct esthetic preferences that at first glance seem alien to a Terran reader. The *paq'batlh* illustrates some of these preferences that are often expressed in the form of proverbs. Some of them have been collected by Marc Okrand in his seminal work *The Klingon Way: A Warrior's Guide*.[21] By briefly explaining the context and meaning of these sayings we hope to partially bridge the cultural gap that remains between a Terran and Klingon readership.

*qa' wIje'meH maSuv*
"We fight to enrich the spirit"

Battle and confrontation occupy a place in Klingon culture very different from ours. For a Klingon, the act of battle is by definition a euphoric experience. The idea of "enriching the spirit" derives from the idea that a Klingon warrior must earn their way to the afterlife, or Sto-vo-kor, through honorable battles—fought much like Viking warriors in order to enter Valhalla. The path to attaining this honor is a fundamental journey for all Klingons. To experience fighting on the battlefield reminds a Klingon of the meaning of his or her existence. The esthetics of battle and its representation play a significant role in all Klingon art forms. In Klingon storytelling in particular, the objective is to dramatize the experience of battle. A Klingon audience wishes to re-experience the battle through the performance. In Klingon music, beauty is said to be produced from the dramatic impact of two opposing forces. It is the struggle between these forces that creates the dynamic that the Klingon audience appreciates.

---

[21] Marc Okrand, *The Klingon Way: A Warrior's Guide* (New York: Pocket Books, 1996).

*ta'mey Dun bommey Dun*
"Great deeds, great songs"
Klingon culture knows a strong oral tradition of passing on great achievements and key events. The most common and effective way of doing so was through song. The act of singing a "battle song" (*may' bom*) or "tribute song" (*van bom*) is of great importance in Klingon social interaction. Thus, a great event is often referred to as a "deed worthy of song." The point of retelling these stories is to relive the accomplishments. Reliving these moments strengthens the listener and performer's cultural affinity with their past and each other. The libretto of an opera (*bom mu'*) is almost always based on a great event from the past.

*Heghlu'DI' mobbe'lu'chugh QaQqu' Hegh wanI'*
"Death is an experience best shared"
Death in this proverb seems to suggest the idea of the theatrical death, one we are also aware of in our culture. In Klingon opera, however, this death should be experienced by both the performer and the audience, and must eventually be an honorable death. The audience is not separated from the theatrical action by conventions of decorum or "proper" behavior; they are encouraged to actively heighten the intensity of the piece by joining in various parts of the action. It is not uncommon for the audience to be driven to such heights of passion that they break into song during the performance or try to join the performers on stage. The Klingons see the experience of telling a story as something that should invoke the original event, thus the line between the act of narrating the event and the event itself becomes blurred if not disappears entirely.

*yIn DayajmeH 'oy' yISIQ*
"To understand life endure pain"

Pain has a significant role in Klingon culture. To be able to endure pain is a sign of courage and honor. A vivid illustration of this is the so-called *nentay,* a rite of passage ritual that tests the worthiness of an adolescent male who aspires to become a warrior. In this ritual the future warrior must pass through two rows of experienced warriors wielding weapons called painsticks.

# Klingon Orthography and Pronunciation

The Klingon language has a rather asymmetric phoneme inventory, which poses several difficulties for any new learners of the language. Anyone familiar with Terran languages like Hindi or Telugu will recognize the retroflex consonants, and several of the lateral, velar, and uvular consonants can be found in Native American or Caucasian languages. Their combination however is decidedly foreign to any Terran language.

The vowels should not pose a problem for any speaker of a European language. Except for one, they follow the "Italian," open pronunciation: a /a/, e /ɛ/, I /ɪ/, o /o/, u /u/.

Table 1 organizes the Klingon consonants according to the standards of the International Phonetic Association. An extensive pronunciation guide tailored to speakers of the English language may be found in Okrand's *Klingon Dictionary*.[1]

[1] Marc Okrand, *The Klingon Dictionary* (New York: Pocket Books, 1992), 13-17.

|  | Labial | Alveolar | Retroflex | Palatal | Velar | Uvular | Laryngeal |
|---|---|---|---|---|---|---|---|
| Nasal | m (m) | n (n) |  |  | ŋ (ng) |  |  |
| Plosive | pʰ b (p b) | tʰ (t) | ɖ (D) |  |  | qʰ (q) | ʔ (') |
| Fricative | v (v) |  | ʂ (S) |  | x ɣ (H gh) |  |  |
| Affricate |  | tʃ dʒ (ch j) |  |  |  | q͡χ (Q) |  |
| Lateral Affr. |  | tɬ (tlh) |  |  |  |  |  |
| Approximant | w (w) |  |  | j (y) |  |  |  |
| Lat. Approx. |  | l (l) |  |  |  |  |  |
| Trill |  | r (r) |  |  |  |  |  |

*Table 1.* Klingon consonant inventory, standard orthography between parentheses.

# Translator's Note

The *paq'batlh* has a long history as both an oral and, later, a written narrative. The basic elements of the story were repeated, more or less intact, in each rendering, but, as the story was told and retold, each storyteller and scribe added a detail here, a flourish there. It is therefore really a challenge to produce a "definitive translation" of a work that has no single source to translate from. It can be assumed that on the Klingon home world there exists a version of the text that is considered canonical—perhaps several versions. Not having had access to these versions in our reconstruction, however, the best we can do in the translation is to find a style that will convey to human readers the same solemnity and reverence and excitement the Klingon does to Klingon readers. It is, after all, Kahless himself who tells us that he is to be remembered not by his words but by his deeds. In recounting these deeds for a human audience in an accessible way, we strive to honor these deeds.

Among Klingons, the story of the *paq'batlh* is traditionally told in the ancient language, or *no' Hol*. Outside of the

Klingon Empire, very little is known about this language. We have discovered fragments, and these are incorporated into the prologue a little bit, but even they are unsure terms. First of all, they are based on our best-guess interpretations of some inscriptions on ancient manuscripts that are difficult to decipher. It is quite possible some of the guesses are wrong—further data and study will determine that. We know that the name of the book itself, *paq'batlh*, is some form of *no' Hol*. It is grammatically backwards from what we find in modern Klingon (where it would be *batlh paq*, or "honor book"). The character we are rendering with an apostrophe in *paq'batlh* may be a clue to some missing grammatical element in *no' Hol* that may explain the transposition of the words. The same hesitancy goes for the names of the some of the subparts of the text. The rendering of the *no' Hol* words into roman letters is meant to mimic the system used to transliterate modern Klingon, but further study may show that another romanization system may be more revealing.

It should be noted that there are a few phrases of *no' Hol* that have worked their way into modern Klingon for various reasons. For example, when a new commander takes over control of a ship, the induction ceremony concludes with the words *Delaq Do'*, meaning something like "Take your stations." This phrase, which is in *no' Hol*, is never heard in any other context. Contemporary speakers of Klingon know phrases of this sort and consider them to be "odd," and many may even know that they are *no' Hol*, but the phrases are isolated, frozen pieces fused onto the living language. Their existence and use does not mean that *no' Hol* is employed as an everyday means of communication.

## TRANSLATOR'S NOTE

For this book, we have decided to present the story of Kahless in modern Klingon rather than *no' Hol* for a number of reasons. First is the lack of confidence in the rendering of *no' Hol* from the ancient manuscripts, as discussed above. Second, though contemporary Klingon has been a topic of linguistic research on Earth for many years and though there are many students of the language—beginners and experts and everything in between—knowledge of *no' Hol* on this planet is negligible. A presentation in *no' Hol*—in whatever transcription that might be most meaningful—might be of interest to linguists and historians, but most readers, even those fluent in a number of modern Klingon dialects, would have a very hard time understanding the text.

Third, among most Klingons, though not all, *no' Hol* is considered not only an ancient form of language, part of a Klingon's heritage, but actually part of each Klingon's identity. While the use of modern Klingon by non-Klingons is not only encouraged (and is actually seen as a symbol of Klingon power and influence), the use of *no' Hol* by non-Klingons in the wrong context and with the wrong intentions can be considered subversive or even traitorous. To Klingons who share this belief, providing information about *no' Hol* to non-Klingons is giving away, irretrievably, something quintessentially Klingon, a sure way to cause Klingons to lose their culture and distinctiveness—even a bit of their Klingon spirit—and simply blend in with the rest of the inhabitants of the galaxy. It is therefore with greatest caution that we have decided to include the few fragments of *no' Hol* in this publication. We have specifically decided to include only the direct fragments we found, and we have not attempted to supplement the text with other known sources of the same narrative.

In rendering the Klingon text in English, several objectives were kept in mind. The language had to be clear so that the story could be easily understood. It also had to retain the right tone of formality found in the original. The form of language that was used for the *paq'batlh* is not conversational, but is a heightened form of language, one that conveys by its choice of vocabulary and turns of phrase the importance of the story being told. Though the contemporary Klingon version is not as lofty, the English echoes the style that we would expect to find in *no' Hol*. Finally, both the English and modern Klingon texts had to follow the formal conventions of Klingon epic literature. Thus, as is typically the case in Klingon epics, most stanzas consist of three lines, generally of unequal lengths. The occasional stanza that does not follow this convention stands out as being of particular importance.[1] Similarly, there is more repetition found in the English version than there would be in normal conversational English or even most forms of English formal prose or poetry. There are a few words that were not translated at all into English, but appear in an Anglicized version of the modern Klingon. For example, the martial art known as *moQbara'* in modern Klingon is rendered as *mok'bara* in English, there being no English counterpart that would make any sense. Similarly, names of places and names of peoples are left pretty much in their original forms, as are all names of individuals (Kahless for *qeylIS* being the most obvious).

---

1 For example, *paq'raD* 3.10–16.

## Translator's Note

Machine translation or computer-aided translation has been available for years now, translating one language into another with greater or lesser success. For an artistic presentation such as the retelling of a great saga or creating the libretto of an opera, however, a person—human or otherwise—is still needed to make sure the outcome carries the tone, intention, emotion, and connotation of the original, not just the basic meaning of the words. The *paq'batlh* is thus best enjoyed read aloud.

Several members of the Klingon Language Institute helped out in the modern Klingon translation—or in tweaking the translation. I would like to thank the KLI's director, Lawrence M. Schoen, for allowing me access to two recent *qep'a'mey* (conventions) where the manuscript was scrutinized. In particular, it is with a great deal of gratitude that I acknowledge the advice and guidance of KLI members Eric Andeen, Alan Anderson, Rhona Fenwick, Captain Krankor, Mark Shoulson, Agnieszka Solska, Tad Stauffer, Robyn Stewart, and especially Andrew Shull-Miller.

### Concerning the Second Edition

This revised edition of the *paq'batlh* would not exist had it not been for the keen eyes and keener minds of the readers of the original edition. Their cogent comments and questions prompted a second look at the earlier work, and that led to the opportunity to fix some errors (typographical and otherwise), refine some phrasing, and incorporate information about the modern language that had come to light since the original publication. The result is, I hope, an improved telling of this foundational Klingon tale. In addition, with deepest thanks to DeSDu', this edition features not merely a glimpse at *no' Hol*, the ancient language found in the Prologue, but an analysis of this obscure tongue as well.

My greatest debt of gratitude goes to De'vID (David Yonge-Mallo). Without his diligent and meticulous work organizing and tracking and questioning various aspects of the project – and definitely without his persistence – this second edition would not have come about. If any errors or ambiguities remain in the translation, of course, they are mine.

— Marc Okrand, May 2022

The Book of Honor

paq'batlh

# Prologue

lut cherlu'

## Dramatis Personae

Master of the Scream (MOS)
Kanjit (KAN)
Kahless, son of Kanjit (KAH)
Morath, son of Kanjit (MOR)
Molor (MOL)
Molor's Envoy (ENV)
Kahnrah, Patriarch of Qam'Chee (KNR)
The Lady Lukara, daughter of Kahnrah (LUK)
The Old Warrior (WAR)
Kortar, Ruler of Gre'thor (KOR)
All present in the arena (incl. audience) (ALL)

## lutvaD ghotvam luDalu'

jachwI'na'
qanjIt
qeylIS qanjIt puqloD
moratlh qanjIt puqloD
molor
molor Duy
qanra' qamchly qup'a'
luqara' qanra' puqbe'
SuvwI' qan
qortar ghe'tor che'wI'
Hoch

## 1. The End

It began with destruction of everything,
    Energy, gods, matter,
    Everything will eventually destroy itself.


They forged a heart
    [From] fire and metal,
    [And called(?) it] Klingon.


... [It was] unchallenged,

    [Thus] a second heart was forged.
... challenged ...

    ...... battle between them.
    Their power combined, invincible,
    They destroyed the gods.

## 1. Dor

tog'Det q'uty 'qootlit
    q'usru Dya 'qinmaa Dya q'op Dya at
    q'uty 'qoot'ag'

[*lacuna of ± 3 lines*]

teq 'qinmaa tyanmuq'
    qil Dya bosru Dya [...]
    tlhengon [...]

[*lacuna of ± 3 lines*]

[......] tubba'lit
.  .  .  .  .  .  .  .  .
    [...] teq tyot lityanmuq'
[...] qoD [...]
.  .  .  .  .  .  .  .  .
    [......] 'ug'ubtyiq
netabq'ot q'usrutyeDi pog' 'eDyayloq'
    'qinmaa me'qoot

[*last line missing?*]

## 2. The Void

Now the two hearts knew emptiness.


The hearts fought the storm,
    The louder they beat,
        The larger the storm became.


    The wind does not respect a fool.
The hearts created [five] forms of *mok'bara*\*
    ... obeyed ...
    The heart above all others.
A Klingon must listen
    To his hearts
    [And] the whispers of his blood.

---

\* Mok'bara (*moQbara'*; *no' Hol: mu'qberet*) is a form of Klingon martial arts. See *paq'raD* 3, note ad loc.

## 2. pagh

Doq' tyemtoq'g'oty tyo teqmaa sye'q
. . . . . . . . . .
. . . . . . . . . .
syisi teqmaa lig'ub
   'ach juqmut wob g'irDet
   Dyav q'usru g'ir Dya
. . . . . . . . . .
. . . . . . . . . .
   quq' syisi vivbat
[...] mu'qberet tunsroot teqmaa metyanmuq'
   [...] lub [...]
   teq nev
teqmaaDoDi jotlhDet
   [...] 'ewDoDi tlhipDet
   tlhengon 'eDinesru

### 3. The Beginning

Out of the end
    Came the beginning,
    … creation.


… they fought
    A fierce battle,
    Matter around them became solid.


They called the place
    Below their feet Paradise.[*]

---

[*] This is one of the few instances a Klingon concept of Paradise (*QI'tu'*; *no' Hol: 'qi'tu'*) appears; see the addendum to Okrand, *The Klingon Dictionary*.

## 3. tagh

Durmut
    tog'
    tyan [...]

[lacuna of ± 9 lines]

[...] 'ulil
    moy' qitqitmut
    q'op srim sribtyuq'

[lacuna of ± 3 lines]

qom bengDoq 'uq'bug' Doq lipung
    'qi'tu' lipung

[last line missing?]

LUT CHERLU'

*Figs.* 1a–c: TL-A, the musical score for the story "The Fool and the Wind" (*qoH SuS je*).

Ground Book

paq'yav

## Prologue

MOS  Hear now,
    All of you here,
    Proud warriors of Kronos[*]
The ways of Kahless,
    For they are true
    And unforgettable.
Hear now,
    All of you here,
    Of the life and death
Of one who fought
    Against the odds,
    And even Gods.
Hear now,
    All of you here,
    Why we go to Sto-vo-kor[†]
And greet our Kahless there,
    To join him in battle
    For eternity.
To join him in battle,
    Join him in battle
    For eternity.
We meet our Kahless there,
    To join him for eternity,
    For eternity.

---

[*] Kronos (*Qo'noS*) is the homeworld of the Klingons, first visited by humans in 2151 CE; cf. MA, s.v. "Qo'noS." It is located in the Klingon System in the Beta Quadrant, about four days away from the Solar System at warp 4.5 (cf. ENT:1X01).

[†] Sto-vo-kor (*Suto'vo'qor*) is the afterlife for the honored dead, created by Kortar (*qortar*; see *paq'QIH* 4.11). It can be compared to the Terran afterlife Valhalla; cf. MA, s.v. "Sto-vo-kor."

## lut cherlu'*

naDev Sughompu'  1
   'ej Qo'noS SuvwI'pu' Hem tlhIH
   qeylIS tIghmey'e'
DaH tIQoy
   teH tIghmey  5
   'ej bIH bolIjlaHbe'†
naDev Sughompu'
   yIn lutDaj'e'
   Hegh lutDaj'e' je
DaH tIQoy  10
   ghaytanHa' QapDI' SuvtaH
   Qunpu' Suvpu'
naDev Sughompu'
   Suto'vo'qor wIghoSmeH ngoQmaj'e'
   DaH tIQoy  15
pa' qeylISma' wIvan
   nItebHa' maSuv
   Hochlogh maSuv
nItebHa' maSuv
   Hochlogh maSuv  20
   nItebHa' maSuv
Hochlogh maSuv
   pa' qeylISma' wIvan
   Hochlogh wItlhej

---

\* In o, the prologue is referred to as "beginning" (*bI'reS*), whereas *lut cherlu'* means "the story is established." Throughout the *paq'batlh*, the titles are tentative, as most of the cantos do not carry "official" titles.

† The prologue features a variation on the Kahless's (*qeylIS*) well-known epithet "unforgettable" (*bolIjlaHbe'*); cf. *paq'QIH* 5.1: *qeylIS lIjlaHbogh pagh*).

## 1. The Hunt

MOS  See the spy creeping,
    He will feed on the weak-hearted,
    See the *targ*,* an easy prey.
Morath, as you failed to kill your prey,
    So will Molor fail to conquer his.
    Kahless, be aware of danger in all forms.
Kahless, pull your *d'k tahg*,†
    Kill the beasts in this forest,
    One a *targ*, and two who call themselves Klingon.

---

\* A *targ* (*targh*) is a herding animal native to Kronos, comparable in form to a Terran boar, but covered with bone spikes. They are both domesticated and hunted for sport.

† A *d'k tahg* (*Daqtagh*) is a traditional Klingon warrior's knife, consisting of a single, straight-edged primary blade and two curved secondary blades, used for hand-to-hand combat; cf. MA, s.v. "d'k tagh."

## 1. wam[*]

ghoS ghoqwI' tam 'e' yItu'  1
   yoHHa'wI' Sop ghaH
   Hub'eghbe' targh
gheDlIj DaHoHHa'pu' moratlh
   'ej gheDDaj charghHa' molor  5
   Qob qo' qeylIS yIqIm
DaqtaghlIj yIQIq qeylIS
   ngemvamDaq Ha'DIbaHmey tIHoH
   wa' targh cha' tlhInganpu'qoq je

---

[*] This first canto of the *paq'yav* is absent in o. In the reconstruction as performed by the KTRE, "The Hunt" (*wam*, lit. "they hunt") was interpreted as a musical introduction, "Hunting Theme" (*chon loDnI'pu'*, lit. "the brothers hunt"). Several sentences can be reconstructed from a popular Klingon children's song featuring elements from the *paq'batlh*.

## 2. Humiliation

KAH  My brother, you failed to kill,
    The head is my reward,
    You bring the carcass home.
This way you will feel
    The burden of shame
    On you and your House.

MOR  One day, brother Kahless,
    You will bow for me
    As leader of our House.
One day, brother Kahless,
    You will not be laughing,
    One day, one day, one day!

## 2. tuH[*]

loDnI'wI' bIHoHta'be'  1
   popwIj 'oH nach'e'
   juHDaq porgh Daqem
vaj
   bItuHqu' SoH  5
   tuqlIj tuHmoHlu'

qeylIS loDnI'
   'opleS chovan
   tuqmaj vIDevmo'
qeylIS loDnI'  10
   'opleS bIHaghbe'
   'opleS 'opleS 'opleS

---

[*]   In 0, the order of the stanzas in canto 2 has been changed to render the conversation more lively: stanza 1 is followed by 3, and 2 by 4.

### 3. The Offer

MOR   What is an envoy of Molor,
      Son of Markag, doing in these woods?
      You are far away from home, stranger.

ENV   You speak wise words,
      The people of the Saq'sub* will be proud
      Of a leader like you.
How would you like
      To keep that promise,
      very soon?
Open the gates for us,
      I can offer you your House
      And your kin will die with honor.

MOR   I will consider your offer,
      You give me the House
      And no blood will be shed.

ENV   Decide when the *qa'rol*† cries,
      The choice is yours,
      And it is obvious.

---

\* The Saq'sub (*SaqSub*) is the native region of Kahless and the location of his estate on Kronos.

† A *qa'rol* is a member of the phylum of birds (*bo'Degh*), larger than a *notqa'*, which is described as a "large, black bird (nowhere near as large as a *qa'rol*, which is really big)" (*HolQeD* 10:4, 4).

## 3. nobqang\*

qatlh ngemDaq ghaHtaH  1
   molor Duy'e' marqagh puqloD'e'
   Hop juHlIj nov

bIjatlhDI' bIchul
   Hem SaqSubnganpu'  5
   DevwI'chaj SoHmo'
tugh
   'Ipvetlh Dapab
   DaneH'a'
maHvaD lojmItmey tIpoSmoH  10
   SoHvaD tuqlIj vInoblaH
   batlh Hegh pal'arpu'lI'

qech Dachupbogh vIqel
   jIHvaD tuq Danobchugh
   'Iw leghbe'lu'  15

jachDI' qa'rol yIwuq
   nIteb bIwuqnIS
   ngeD Qu'vam

---

\* Canto 3 appears in o in a largely different form. It opens with Morath (*moratlh*) becoming aware of Molor (disguised as an envoy), and addressing him directly.

### 4. Waiting for Death to Come

MOS   They sneak and they creep,
      The men of mighty Molor,
      Like beasts in the dark.

ALL   In the Saq'sub all is quiet,
      Its warriors asleep, like children
      Waiting for death to come
  In their homes, in their homes,
      Waiting for death to come,
      Death to come.

MOS   Then the *qa'rol* raises voice,
      The signal for Morath
      To lose his pride and claim a throne.
  He leaves his kin, unlocks the gates,
      The army closes in, smelling blood.
      Oh, Morath, and you know this:

ALL   In the Saq'sub all is quiet,
      Its warriors asleep, like children
      Waiting for death to come
  In their homes, in their homes,
      Waiting for death to come,
      Death to come.

## 4. Heghrup loSlI'[*]

ghoStaHvIS tam 'ej So''egh 1
   molor QaS HoS
   ram Ha'DIbaHmey rur

SaqSubDaq pagh Qoylu'
   Qong SuvwI'pu' puqpu' rur 5
   Heghrup loSlI'
juH qachchajDaq juH qachchajDaq
   Heghrup loSlI'
   Heghrup

ghIq jach qa'rol 10
   maQ 'oH
   HemHa'choH 'ej cho'choH moratlh
pal'arpu'Daj lon lojmIt ngaQHa'moH
   SumchoH mangghom 'Iw largh
   moratlh wanI'vam DaSov 15

SaqSubDaq pagh Qoylu'
   Qong SuvwI'pu' puqpu' rur
   Heghrup loSlI'
juH qachchajDaq juH qachchajDaq
   Heghrup loSlI' 20
   Heghrup

---

[*] Canto 4 has a classical chorus structure (*cha'ang*), with the audience replying to the Master of the Scream.

MOS  Then fires burst under the roofs
    Of the Saq'sub's ancient houses,
      Flames have no mercy for anyone.
Morath knows he has been a fool,
    His promised kingdom will be ash
    By the time he claims the sword.
How does a coward claim a sword?
    By taking it from his sleeping father.
    So he did, so he did, so he did.
Morath wakes his father,
    The old Kanjit,
    His hearts[*] weak, but proud.

ALL  In the Saq'sub all is quiet,
    Its warriors asleep, like children
    Waiting for death to come
In their homes, in their homes,
    Waiting for death to come,
    Death to come.

---

[*] Klingons have a redundancy in internal organs known as *brak'lul* (*bIraqlul*) and have an eight-chambered heart (see TNG:5x16). Due to this redundancy, Klingons are sometimes said to have two hearts, though this may be medically inaccurate; cf. the scene in which Kahless takes out Molor's hearts (*paq'raD* 46–48).

SaqSub qach tIQ beb bIngDaq
   pay' qul'a' tu'lu'
   HochvaD pung Hutlh qul
Dogh ghaH 'e' Sov moratlh             25
   'etlh DoQDI'
   meQchu'pu' wo' che'rupbogh
chay' 'etlh DoQ nuch
   QongtaHbogh qup 'etlh nIH
   vaj nIHpu' vaj nIHpu' vaj nIHpu'       30
qanjIt qan vemmoH moratlh
   vavDaj ghaH qanjIt'e'
   puj tIqDu'Daj 'ach Hem

SaqSubDaq pagh Qoylu'
   Qong SuvwI'pu' puqpu' rur           35
   Heghrup loSlI'
juH qachchajDaq juH qachchajDaq
   Heghrup loSlI'
   Heghrup

## 5. Father and Son

MOR  Surrender, father,
    Surrender while you can.
    Surrender, or we'll die.

KAN  I see now, I have failed
    To raise my son a man.
    Water flows through his veins.
Morath, you coward!
    Give me my sword
    And get out of my way.
Do not resist, me, son.
    Father and son fighting,
    There is nothing worse.

MOR  Old man!
    What do you know?
    I will fight you if I must!

KAN  You have water running through your veins!
    Give it to me,
    I command you!

MOR  There will be
    Nothing to command,
    Ever again!

## 5. vav puqloD je

yIjegh vavwI'  1
   bIjeghlaHtaHvIS
   bIjeghbe'chugh vaj maHegh

SuvwI' DameH puqloDwI'
   vIghojHa'moH DaH 'e' vItlhoj  5
   bIQ lungaS 'aDDu'Daj
nuch SoH moratlh
   jIHvaD 'etlhwIj yInob
   ghIq yImej
HIqaDQo' puqloDwI'  10
   SuvchuqDI' vav puqloD je
   wanI' Do'Ha' law' Hoch Do'Ha' puS

loD qan
   nuq DaSov
   qaghobnISchugh maghobchuq  15

bIQ lungaS 'aDDu'lIj
   yInob
   qara'

not
   vay'  20
   Dara'qa'

### 6. Father's Death

MOS  What is this?
    I wake up to the sound
    Of battle between my kin!

KAN  My son, I have failed,
    I've raised you without honor,
    Go now, leave me.
And get your brother,
    Molor must be stopped
    Go, go, go!

KAH  You did not raise me a coward,
    I will prove it to you,
    Go now, to Gre'thor.*
Your honor will be saved,
    I will return to this house
    Victorious! Victorious! Victorious!
Morath!
    I will hunt you down!
    *P'takh! P'takh! P'takh!*†

---

\*   Gre'thor (*ghe'tor*) is the Klingon Underworld, ruled by Kortar. The gates of Gre'thor are guarded by Fek'lhr (*veqlargh*); cf. *paq'yav* 11.11; MA, s.v. "Gre'thor."

†   P'takh (*petaQ*) is an insulting Klingon epithet. Its resemblance to the verb *taQ*, meaning "be weird", preceded by the you (plural) imperative prefix (*pe-*) is coincidental, and the claim that they are related is not supported by research.

## 6. Hegh vav

qaStaH nuq  
   ghobchuq pal'arpu'wI'  
   muvemmoH may' wab

puqloDwI' jIlujpu'  
   bInenchoHpu' 'ach quv DaHutlh  
   yIghoS yImej  
'ej loDnI'lI' yIjon  
   molor DaQapbe'nISmoH  
   yIghoS yIghoS yIghoS

quv vIHutlhbe'  
   nuch jIHbe' 'e' vItob  
   DaH ghe'tor yIghoS  
quvlIj vIchoq  
   qachvam vIcheghDI' charghwI' jIH  
   yay yay yay  
moratlh  
   qaSambej  
   petaQ petaQ petaQ

## 7. The Pursuit

MOS
The brothers ran
    From their home,
    Neither one gives up.
Running
    Over the Black Hills
    Until Kri'stak* blocks their path.

---

\* The Kri'stak (*QIStaq*) volcano plays a major role in the *paq'batlh* as the place where Kahless forges his *bat'leth* sword at the end of the *paq'yav*; cf. MA, s.v. "Kri'stak volcano." It is also the entrance to Gre'thor; cf. *paq'yav* 11.9.

## 7. tlha'*

juHchajvo'  1
   qet loDnI'pu'
   taH chaH
HuDqIjDaq
   qet  5
   ghIq Hechaj bot QIStaq

---

\* Like the first canto, this text of this canto is absent from o and was interpreted musically as the "Chase Theme" (*qet chaH*, lit. "they run")

## 8. Prelude to the Fight

KAH  Now, Morath
     You can run no more,
     Your legs are weak.
As are your hearts
     Filled with water,
     All blood is lost.
This is the end,
     Give me the sword,
     For you know it is mine.

## 8. Suvrup

moratlh
   DaH bIHaw'laHtaHbe'
   puj 'uSDu'lIj
bIQ lungaS
   tIqDu'lIj
   loj 'Iw luHutlhbej
pItlh
   'etlh HInob
   'etlhwIj 'oH 'etlh'e' 'e' DaSov

## 9. Battle of the Brothers

ALL  Twelve days, twelve nights,
    Twelve days, twelve nights,
    Twelve days, twelve nights.

MOS  They fought on and on,
    The sand beneath their feet
    Turned hard as rock.

ALL  Twelve days, twelve nights,
    Twelve days, twelve nights,
    Twelve days, twelve nights.

MOS  Their anger so hot,
    It could melt the rock
    Like the mighty Kri'stak.

ALL  Twelve days, twelve nights,
    Twelve days, twelve nights,
    Twelve days, twelve nights.

MOS  And Morath's strength was gone,
    The coward threw his sword
    Into the fire streams of Kri'stak.

ALL  Twelve days, twelve nights,
    Twelve days, twelve nights,
    Twelve days, twelve nights.

## 9. ghobchuq loDnI'pu'[*]

wa'maH cha' pem wa'maH cha' ram  1
   wa'maH cha' pem wa'maH cha' ram
   wa'maH cha' pem wa'maH cha' ram

SuvtaH SuvtaH
   qamDu'chaj bIngDaq  5
   letchoH lam nagh rur

wa'maH cha' pem wa'maH cha' ram
   wa'maH cha' pem wa'maH cha' ram
   wa'maH cha' pem wa'maH cha' ram

tujqu'choHmo' QeHchaj  10
   nagh tetlaH tujvam
   QIStaq HoS rur

wa'maH cha' pem wa'maH cha' ram
   wa'maH cha' pem wa'maH cha' ram
   wa'maH cha' pem wa'maH cha' ram  15

ghIq HoSHa'choHpu' moratlh
   QIStaq qul bIQtIqHomDaq
   'etlhDaj vo' nuch

wa'maH cha' pem wa'maH cha' ram
   wa'maH cha' pem wa'maH cha' ram  20
   wa'maH cha' pem wa'maH cha' ram

---

[*] Part of the musical score of canto 9 has also been located on TL-B; see fig. 2, *infra*.

MOS  And Kahless dropped his sword
         To kill the traitor with bare hands,
         Morath felt the end was near.

ALL  Twelve days, twelve nights,
         Twelve days, twelve nights,
         Twelve days, twelve nights.

MOS  Morath the coward
         Jumped after his sword,
         Dishonored and defeated.

ALL  Twelve days, twelve nights,
         Twelve days, twelve nights,
         Twelve days, twelve nights.

MOS  And Kahless was alone
         Walking along the shore,
         His fate heavy on his shoulders.
     Kahless sits at the shores
         Of the lake of fire
         As an old warrior passes by.

'urwI' HoHmeH ghopDu'Daj neH lo'meH qeylIS
   'etlhDaj chagh
   tugh Hegh 'e' Sov moratlh

wa'maH cha' pem wa'maH cha' ram
   wa'maH cha' pem wa'maH cha' ram
   wa'maH cha' pem wa'maH cha' ram

nuch ghaH moratlh'e'
   quvHa' moratlh 'ej jeylu'pu'
   'etlhDaj tlha'

wa'maH cha' pem wa'maH cha' ram
   wa'maH cha' pem wa'maH cha' ram
   wa'maH cha' pem wa'maH cha' ram

mob qeylIS
   ngeng HeHDaq yIt
   SanDaj buS vaj 'It
qul ngeng HeHDaq
   ba'taHvIS qeylIS
   ghoS SuvwI' qan

## 10. Kahless and the Old Warrior

WAR  My Klingon brother,
    Why are you out here,
    Where even the *thranx*[*] don't grow?
Can I help a fellow Klingon in need?
    May I sit
    And rest with you?

KAH  Dear old friend,
    I cannot speak of my tragedies,
    There is nothing left for me.

WAR  If you don't want my help,
    Then let's light a fire and drink,
    Have some bloodwine[†]!

KAH  Let us drink then
    To my father in Gre'thor
    And the brother I once had.

WAR  You are here for great deeds,
    Your journey will not be forgotten,
    Restore the honor of your father.
To reach the heavens,
    You must seek underground,
    I will see you victorious next time.

---

[*] The *thranx* plant (*tlheng'IQ*) mentioned is an indigenous Klingon plant which only flowers every eight years; cf. Michael-Jan Friedman, *Kahless* (New York: Pocket Books, 1997), 60.

[†] Bloodwine (*'Iw HIq*) is a Klingon alcoholic beverage, twice as strong as whisky and commonly served warm; cf. MA, s.v. "bloodwine."

## 10. qeylIS SuvwI' qan je

tlhIngan loDnI'wI'  1
   qatlh naDev SoHtaH
   naDev taHbe' tlheng'IQ
tlhIngan Do'Ha' vIQaHlaH'a'
   jIba' 'ej qatlhej 'e' Dachaw''a'  5
   jIleS 'ej qatlhej 'e' Dachaw''a'

wIj jup
   SengmeywIj vIja'laHbe'
   jIHvaD ratlh pagh

qaQaH DaneHbe'chugh  10
   vaj qul wIchenmoH 'ej matlhutlh
   'Iw HIq yItlhutlh

vaj matlhutlhjaj
   ghe'torDaq ghaHtaHbogh vavwI''e' wIquvmoHjaj
   Heghbogh loDnI'wI' wIquvmoHjaj!  15

ta'mey Dun Data'meH naDev SoHtaH
   bIve' net lIjbe'
   quvqa'meH vavlI' yIvang
chalDaq DapawmeH
   wutlhDaq bInejnIS
   qaleghqa'DI' charghwI' SoH

### 11. Kahless Enters Gre'thor

MOS The old man walks away,
    Then dawn lights the surroundings,
    Kahless is at the entrance of Gre'thor.
He understands now
    The wise words
    Of the old man.
Kahless enters Gre'thor,
    Follows the river of fire
    Deep into the Kri'stak volcano.
One can only return from this Underworld,
    If Fek'lhr* does not notice one
    Entering or leaving Gre'thor.
No one has ever succeeded.
    Walking along the banks
    In the heart of Kri'stak,
Kahless finds himself in a cave
    Leading to
    The world beyond the living.

---

\* Fek'lhr (*veqlargh*) is the guardian of Gre'thor, the Klingon Underworld; cf. MA, s.v. "Fek'lhr."

## 11. ghe'tor 'el qeylIS

mej loD qan 1
   qaS jajlo' wovchoH chal
   ghe'tor DInDaq ghaHtaH qeylIS'e'
DaH
   loD qan mu'mey chul 5
   yaj
ghe'tor 'el qeylIS
   qul bIQtIqDaq ghoS
   QIStaq qoD ghoS
ghe'tor 'el nuv qoj ghe'tor mej ghaH 10
   'e' tu'be'chugh neH veqlargh
   ghe'torvo' cheghlaH nuvvam
not Qapta' vay'
   QIStaq qoD 'el qeylIS
   bIQtIq HeHDaq yIttaHvIS 15
DIS 'elpu' 'e' tlhoj
   DISvam veghlu'chugh
   yInbogh nuvpu' Hutlhbogh qo'Daq pawlu'

### 12. Kahless Forges the *Bat'leth*\*

KAH  I am made for great deeds,
>    I must take control
>    Of myself, my surroundings, everything!

ALL  Sparks from the fire river
>    Caught his hair,
>    Caught his hair.

KAH  Fearless, I will be,
>    Ruthless, I will strike,
>    Rational and planned.

ALL  Caught his hair
>    And turned to steel
>    Before his eyes.

KAH  I will save my kin
>    From Gre'thor
>    And take revenge!

---

\* Kahless is commonly credited with forging the first *bat'leth* (*betleH*), meaning "sword of honor" (cf. MA, s.v. "bat'leth"), an archaic formation containing the roots for "honor" (*batlh*) and "sword" (*'etlh*), by cutting a lock from his hair and dropping it in the lava of the Kri'stak volcano (cf. TNG:6x23). In the *paq'batlh* this scene is depicted in the lyric chorus style (*cha'ang*) and suggests that the sparks from the lava caught Kahless's hair, turning into the steel of the *bat'leth*. A traditional *bat'leth* is about 116 cm long, weighing about 5.3 kg. The blades are forged from baakonite, a Klingon metal alloy (cf. DS9:2x19).

## 12. betleH chenmoH qeylIS

ta'mey Dun vIta'rup jISeH'eghnIS 1
   muDechbogh Dochmey vISeHnIS
   Hoch vISeHnIS

jIbDaj lumeQmoH
   jIbDaj lumeQmoH 5
   qul bIQtIq qulHommey

jIyoHqu'
   jInaS jImupDI'
   jImeq jInab

jIbDaj lumeQmoH 10
   'ej bejtaHvIS
   baS moj jIb

ghe'torDaq lengbe'meH
   pal'arpu'wI' vIQan
   muyonmoH bortaS neH 15

PAQ'YAV

Figs. 2a-c: TL-B, the musical score for *paq'yav* 9,
"The Battle of the Brothers" (*ghobchuq loDnI'pu'*).

Force Book

paq'raD

## Prologue

MOS  Kahless, Kahless, Kahless,
       Now forge the *bat'leth*,
       Weapon of pride.

ALL  Go, Kahless, go, go down!
       Grip your *bat'leth*
       And let it guide your blood.

MOS  Now Kahless continues,
       Armed and ready,
       Past the heart of Kri'stak.
  It ends at a cliff,
       Leading straight into the core
       Of Kronos

ALL  Go, Kahless, go, go down!
       Grip your *bat'leth*
       And let it guide your blood.

MOS  And Kahless fell
       For eternity, it seemed,
       In never ending darkness.
  Then he sees bright red
       At the end of his fall
       It is a river, blood-colored.

## lut cherlu'

qeylIS qeylIS qeylIS  
   DaH betleH yIchenmoH  
   batlh nuH yIchenmoH

yIghIr qeylIS yIghIr  
   betleHlIj yI'uch  
   'IwlIj Devjaj*

DaH QIStaq botlh juStaH qeylIS  
   nuHmey ghaj  
   'ej Suvrup ghaH  
bIQtIq qa'rI'Daq pawDI' qeylIS  
   qojDaq Qam  
   bIngDaq Qo'noS SuqSIv legh

yIghIr qeylIS yIghIr  
   betleHlIj yI'uch  
   'IwlIj Devjaj

'ej pum qeylIS  
   pumtaH HurghtaH  
   pumtaH HurghtaH  
ghIq pum 'e' mev  
   bIQtIq Doq legh  
   bIQtIq nguvmoH 'Iw

---

\*   Of the second stanza (and fifth and ninth), an alternative Klingon reading has been attested in o: *yIghoS qeylIS yIghoS yIghIr/ betleHlI' yI'uchchu'/ 'ej 'IwlIj Devjaj betleHlI'*.

MOS  The blood streams carry him
(CONT.)  To the great gates of Gre'thor,
  The land from where none return.

ALL  Go, Kahless, go, go down!
  Grip your *bat'leth*
  And let it guide your blood.

ghe'tor lojmIt'a'Daq 22
    'Iw bIQtIq ghoS
    naDevvo' chegh pagh

 25
yIghIr qeylIS yIghIr
    betleHlIj yI'uch
    'IwlIj Devjaj

### 1. The Deceit of Fek'lhr

MOS  Kahless, Kahless, Kahless!
     At the gates of Gre'thor,
     Here you are.
Those unfit disintegrate
     At the glance of Fek'lhr,
     So it is said.
No one knows for sure,
     Many have entered,
     None have returned.
The fearless warrior
     Climbs out of the blood
     Onto dry land.
Strange sounds come from afar,
     It is the Barge of the Dead,
     With Kortar at its helm.
Kortar, Kortar, Kortar!
     Guide our warriors
     To their final battleground.
Kahless knows by instinct
     A fight will not suffice
     To enter the land of the dead.
The lights from the ship
     Reflect on his *bat'leth*,
     Soon Kahless will devise a plan.
The spirits of the dead
     Go to the gates of Gre'thor
     In lines of three.

## 1. veqlargh toj

qeylIS qeylIS qeylIS    1
  ghe'tor lojmItDaq
  SoHtaH
nuv 'umHa' leghchugh veqlargh
  ngoS nuv 'umHa'    5
  jatlhlu'
Sovbej pagh
  'elta' nuv law'
  cheghta' pagh
'Iw bIQtIqvo'    10
  toS SuvwI' yoH
  puH QaDDaq\* paw
Daq SumHa'vo' wab Huj Qoylu'
  Hegh Dujvo' wab Qoylu'
  DeghwI' ghaH qortar'e'    15
qortar qortar qortar
  che'ronchaj QavDaq
  SuvwI'pu'ma' tIDev
QaQ qeylIS Duj
  ghe'tor 'elmeH    20
  yapbe' may' 'e' Sovchu'
qeylIS betleH bochvo'
  'et Duj wovmoHwI'mey
  tugh nab 'ogh qeylIS
ghe'tor lojmIt    25
  lughoS Heghpu'bogh nuvpu' qa'pu'
  chen wej tlheghmey

---

\* The word *QaD* literally means "be dry," but has a slang meaning of "be safe, protected." See Marc Okrand, *Klingon for the Galactic Traveler* (New York: Pocket Books, 1997), 161.

MOS   Fek'lhr inspects them,
(CONT.)      One by one,
        With his deadly glance.
    Kahless, Kahless, Kahless!
       Beware those eyes
       For they will kill without a doubt.
    When the eyes of death are upon him,
       Light reflects off the *bat'leth*
       Into Fek'lhr's evil eyes.
    His eyes are blinded for a while,
       And Kahless enters Gre'thor
       Unharmed and safe.

QIt wa' qa' nuD veqlargh 28
  QIt latlh qa' nuD veqlargh
    Hegh lurur mInDu'Daj 30
qeylIS qeylIS qeylIS
  Qob mInDu'vetlh
    HoHbej bIH
lubejtaHvIS Heghna' mInDu'
  betleHvo' veqlargh mInDu' mIghDaq 35
    'et tamghay
qaStaHvIS poH ngaj leghlaHbe'
  ghe'tor 'el qeylIS
    rIQbe' ghaH 'ej QaD

## 2. A Brother's Forgiveness[*]

KAH My brother, I see your anger,
    You might have a chance
    To make amends.
I am as alive as I was
    When you left me at Kri'stak,
    I have an offer to make.
Come, come, come
    With me to the living,
    And fight Molor with me.
In battle, you will die with honor,
    So you can give yourself to Kortar
    As a hero of the Klingon tribes.

MOR What a fool I have been,
    Blinded by fear and spite,
    And still you find me worthy.
This can only mean
    Our family bonds are stronger
    Than even death itself.
Brother, on this day I swear
    To be honorable and die
    In battle, fighting against Molor.

---

[*] The translation of the Klingon title is literally "A Brother Un-resents." The concept of forgiveness is considered very "un-Klingon"; cf. for example the title of this canto in 0, which similarly excludes any notion of "forgiveness": *loDnI'Daj quvqa'moH*, lit. "he causes the brother to have honor again."

## 2. qeHHa' loDnI'

| | |
|---|---|
| loDnI'wI' | 1 |
|   bIQeHba' | |
|   chaq batlh bIvangqa'laH | |
| QIStaqDaq cholonDI' jIyIn | |
|   DaH jIyIn je | 5 |
|   SoHvaD jIchup | |
| yIntaHbogh nuvpu'Daq | |
|   HItlhej HItlhej HItlhej | |
|   'ej nItebHa' molor wISuv | |
| bIHarghtaHvIS batlh bIHegh | 10 |
|   vaj qortarvaD bInob'eghDI' | |
|   tlhIngan tuqmey Sub SoH | |

| | |
|---|---|
| jIDoghqu' | |
|   vIghIjlu'mo' 'ej bortaS vIneHmo' | |
|   jIleghlaHbe' 'ach chovuvtaH | 15 |
| vaj | |
|   qorDu'maj ruS HoS law' | |
|   Hegh HoS puS | |
| loDnI' DaHjaj | |
|   batlh jIvang 'e' vI'Ip | 20 |
|   molor vISuvtaHvIS jIHegh | |

### 3. The Family Reunites

KAH  I will show you now
>  The forms of the *mok'bara*,*
>  So we can reunite in the flesh.
>  Let us join our mind and body
>  In the forms of the *mok'bara*,
>  To reunite body and soul.

KAN+MOR  We are ready,
>  Let us commence
>  This ancient rite.

KAH  First *Nach*, the form of the head,
>  Then *Ghiv*, the form of the legs and arms,
>  Then *Burgh*, the form of the stomach,†
>  Then *Bing*, the form of the space below,
>  And *Dung*, the space above,
>  And finally *Tiq*, the heart and center of all things,
>  May it forever beat, anywhere.

---

\*  *Mok'bara* (*moQbara'*) is a Klingon form of martial arts, and the basis of hand-to-hand combat techniques. It can also be deployed in combination with weapons, such as the *bat'leth*; cf. MA, s.v. "mok'bara." It remains uncertain whether Kahless invented *mok'bara* or merely transmitted the techniques that existed before him. However, he must definitely be credited with combining the martial art form with swordplay.

†  In English, the word "stomach" may refer to the midsection of the body (belly, abdomen) or else the internal organ. In Klingon "belly" and "stomach (organ)" are two different words; *chor* and *burgh*. However, as an exception, we believe *burgh* here is used to refer to both the organ and the midsection of the body. As this passage is from the O: libretto source material, we believe the use of the word "stomach" here could be attributed to artistic license on the part of the librettists.

## 3. ghomchuqqa' loDnI'pu' vav je

maghomchuqqa'DI' SuyInbejmeH 1
   DaH moQbara' tonSaw'mey
   Sa'agh
muvchuqqa'meH porgh qa' je
   muvchuqjaj yabmaj porghmaj je 5
   moQbara' tonSaw' DIlo'taHvIS

SuH
   tayvam tIQ
   wIlopchoHjaj

wa'DIch nach 'ay' 10
   cha'DIch ghIv 'ay'
   wejDIch burgh 'ay'
   loSDIch bIng 'ay'
   vaghDIch Dung 'ay'
   tagha' tIq Hoch Dochmey qolqoS 15
   Hochlogh Dat joqtaHjaj*

---

\* The third stanza of canto 3 has an anomalous metrical structure, most probably owing to its ritual function. Also, TL-A features a different fourth and fifth line: *loSDIch Hugh 'ay' / vaghDIch SoQ 'ay'*. *Hugh* is the word for "throat." *SoQ* seems to be an ancient word meaning "space beside."

KAN+MOR   We are now connected,
               Spirit and body are one,
               Until our time comes.

KAH   You have both finished
           The forms of the *mok'bara*
           Welcome to this place.

DaH mararchuq  20
   mayIntaHvIS
   muvchuqtaH qa' porgh je

moQbara' 'ay'mey
   bota'ta'
   batlh Daqvam boDab

### 4. The Escape

MOS  And so their spirit and body connected,
    The two warriors resurrect
      to confront Molor.
Kahless and his kin
    Were almost at the gates,
    When Fek'lhr came in.
He screamed: "Where is the p'takh
    Who dares to enter Gre'thor
    Within a body?!
"I will hunt you down
    Like a targ and slay you,
    Then eat both your hearts!"
In his rage, Fek'lhr never saw
    Two of Kortar's souls and Kahless
    Enter the Barge of the Dead.
The next day, the barge set sail
    On the river of blood,
      On its way to gather the souls of the fallen ones.

## 4. nargh

vaj porghchaj muvqa' qa'chaj  1
   molor luqaDmeH
   yInqa' cha' SuvwI'pu'
tlhoS lojmIt vegh
   qeylIS pal'arpu'Daj je  5
   'elDI' veqlargh
jach veqlargh jatlh
   muqaD vay' 'ej ghe'tor 'el porgh
   nuqDaq ghaH petaQ'e'
targh Darur  10
   vaj qaSam 'ej qaHoH
   ghIq cha' tIqDu'lIj vISop
QeHqu'mo' veqlargh
   Hegh Duj lu'el cha' qortar qa'pu' qeylIS je
   'e' leghbe' veqlargh  15
qaSDI' wa'leS
   SuvwI'pu' qa'pu' yIrmeH
   'Iw bIQtIqDaq lengchoH Duj

### 5. Kortar's Rage

ALL   Kortar, Kortar, Kortar!
      Two of your souls are missing,
      You can sense it, but how can it be?

KOR   Fek'lhr! Guardian of my souls,
      You have been outwitted
      By a mere mortal!

ALL   Kortar, Kortar, Kortar!
      Assemble your Qempa'keh,[*]
      The proudest spirits of Gre'thor!

KOR   He has broken the ancient rules,
      He has defied his destiny
      Curse this Klingon, who has no shame!

ALL   Kortar, Kortar, Kortar!
      Assemble your Qempa'keh,
      The proudest spirits of Gre'thor!

KOR   I will bring this *p'takh* to justice
      And teach him life and death,
      The slow and painful way!

ALL   Kortar, Kortar, Kortar!
      Assemble your Qempa'keh,
      The proudest spirits of Gre'thor!

---

[*] The Qempa'keh (*qempa'QeH*) are the enraged (*QeH*) ancestral spirits (*qempa'*) populating Gre'thor.

## 5. QeH qortar

qortar qortar qortar  1
   DachchoH cha' qa'
   'e' Dajem 'ach chay' qaS

veqlargh
   qa'pu'wI' 'avwI'  5
   Dutojta' ghotHom jubbe'

qortar qortar qortar
   qempa'QeHlI' tIghommoH
   ghe'torDaq qa'pu'vam Hem law' Hoch Hem puS

chutmey tIQ wemta'  10
   SanDaj qaDta'
   tuHbe' tlhInganvam jay'

qortar qortar qortar
   qempa'QeHlI' tIghommoH
   ghe'torDaq qa'pu'vam Hem law' Hoch Hem puS  15

petaQvam vIqopbej
   QIt ghaHvaD yIn Hegh je vIghojmoH
   'ej 'oy' SIQ ghaH

qortar qortar qortar
   qempa'QeHlI' tIghommoH  20
   qa'pu'vam Hem law' Hoch Hem puS

KOR Qempa'keh, we will travel
    Up the river of blood
    And bring this traitor down!

qempa'QeH
 'Iw bIQtIqDaq maleng
 'ej 'urwI'vam wIjey

### 6. Forging the Resistance

MOS  Kahless tells his brother and father
    to go their separate ways,
    And travel the lands.
To tell the Klingon tribes
    their story of courage,
    And honor.
To tell them that now is the time
    To take up their arms,
    And fight against Molor.
To tell them that Kahless asks them
    To take up their arms,
    And fight against Molor
To make the Klingon people proud
    And self-sufficient once more,
    And fight with honor!
To remind them that they
    Don't need anyone but themselves,
    For they are Klingon!

## 6. 'omchoH chaH

loDnI'Daj vavDaj je ja' qeylIS                      1
   nIteb peghoS
   HatlhDaq peve'
toDuj lutraj quv lutraj je
   QoymeH tlhIngan tuqmey              5
   tIja'
DaH peHarghchoH
   DaH molor yISuvchoH
   tIja'
molor luSuvmeH                                     10
   nuHmeychaj Suq
   'e' tlhob qeylIS
tlhInganpu' Hemqa'moHmeH
   tlhInganpu' tlhabqa'moHmeH
   batlh Suv 'e' tlhob qeylIS          15
wuv'eghlaH
   boQ lupoQbe'
   tlhIngan chaH

## 7. The Barren Lands

MOS   And Kahless traveled to
     His beloved Saq'sub,
     Over the mountains,
He finds the lands of his father
     Barren and deserted,
     It was alive and prosperous once.
It was as if the spirit of life
     Had forsaken the earth,
     And no one cared about its fate.
Then Kahless arrived at his home,
     Once built by his father's own hands,
     He found it destroyed and desolate.
Molor did not destroy Kahless
     By burning his house
     Or ravaging his lands.
Instead, by doing so,
     Kahless grew mighty and strong,
     And it fueled his will to fight.
To the death, to the death, to the death,
     It fueled his will to fight
     To the death.
Kahless also went out to search
     For allies across Kronos,
     And told them his tale.
All were bemused by his words,
     Wise and full of spirit,
     And astonished to see him alive.

## 7. Deb mojpu' yer

SaqSub'e' muSHa'bogh  1
   pawmeH leng qeylIS
   HuDmey Sal ghIq ghIr
Deb mojpu' vavDaj yer
   'ej choSchoHlu'pu' 'e' tu'  5
   'op ben pa' Dab ngan 'ej chep
puH lonlaw'ta'
   yIn qa'
   SanDaj SaH pagh
ghIq juH qachDajDaq paw qeylIS  10
   qachvam luchenmoHta' vavDaj ghopDu'
   'ach DaH Qaw'lu' 'ej chIm 'e' tu'
qeylIS Qaw' 'e' nIDmeH
   yerDaj weH molor
   'ej juH qachDaj meQmoH  15
'ach luj molor
   vangmo' molor HoSghajchoHqu' qeylIS
   'ej SuvqangmoHbej
Suvchu'meH Suvchu'meH Suvchu'meH
   ghaH SuvqangmoHchu'  20
   molor
Qo'noSDaq boqwI'mey
   nejmeH je ve' qeylIS
   'ej chaHvaD lut jatlh
Hoch qImmoH mu'meyDaj  25
   ghob 'agh 'ej chul
   yIntaH 'e' luleghmo' chaH mer

### 8. Return to the Saq'sub

MOS The Saq'sub lay
    Empty and desolate,
    Under the Praxis* moon.
But when the sun appeared,
    So did Morath and Kanjit,
    Over the hills, they came.
The sun shone not on them only,
    Behind them came
    An army of brave warriors.
On the other side of the land,
    Kahless traveled the lands
    With an equal number of proud Klingons.

ALL All tribes,
    All ages,
    All sexes,
United to do battle together!
    Against the tyrant Molor!
    Against fear and against weakness!

MOS And Kahless spoke to them
    In every village and city he went,
    Filled with pride and authority,
About avenging their stolen pride,
    About caring for their weapons,
    For they represent the purity of their blood.

---

\* Praxis (*pIraqSIS*) was a Klingon moon, which was later exploited as one of the Empire's main energy production facilities. It exploded in 2293 CE owing to over-mining and insufficient safety measures; cf. MA, s.v. "Praxis."

## 8. SaqSub chegh[*]

pIraqSIS maS bIngDaq　　　　　　　　　　　　　1
　　pIgh rur SaqSub chIm
　　choSlu'pu'bogh
'ach narghDI' jul
　　nargh je moratlh qanjIt je　　　　　　　　　　5
　　HuDmeyvo' ghIr chaH
chaH neHHa' wovmoH jul
　　chaH 'emvo' ghoS
　　SuvwI'pu' mangghom yoH
Sepvetlh latlh DopDaq　　　　　　　　　　　　　10
　　Hatlh ve'taHvIS qeylIS
　　lutlhej tlhInganpu' Hem mI' nIb

Hoch tuqmey
　　Hoch puq poHmey
　　Hoch loDpu' be'pu' je　　　　　　　　　　　　15
HarghmeH yeq chaH
　　molor HI''a' luSuv
　　lughIjlu'be' 'ej pujHa' 'e' lu'aghmeH Suv

'ej Hoch vengHomDaq Hoch vengDaq je
　　Suchbogh ghaH qeylIS luQoy　　　　　　　　　20
　　woQ le'yo' je 'aghbej ghaH
le'yo'raj nIHlu'ta'mo' penoD jatlh qeylIS
　　nuHmeyraj tIQorgh
　　watlh 'Iwraj 'e' lu'aghmo' nuHmey jej

---

[*] Canto 8 is also known under the alternate title "Kahless's Speech" (*jatlh qeylIS*).

ALL   All tribes,
      All ages,
      All sexes,
    United to do battle together!
      Against the tyrant Molor!
      Against fear and against weakness!

MOS   After Kahless's words, they celebrate,
      For they may soon die with honor!
      For they may soon be victorious!

Hoch tuqmey 25
   Hoch puq poHmey
   Hoch loDpu' be'pu' je
HarghmeH yeq chaH
   molor HI''a' luSuv
   lughIjlu'be' 'ej pujHa' 'e' lu'aghmeH Suv 30

jatlh 'e' mevDI' qeylIS, lop
   chaq tugh batlh Heghmo'
   'ej chaq tugh charghmo'

### 9. Kortar Learns the Name

MOS  Not far away,
    Kortar and his Qempa'keh
    Are in search for their souls.
Upon reaching the upper world,
    No one could speak of anything,
    But the deeds of Kahless and his kin.
Now Kortar has the name
    Of the one who eluded Fek'lhr,
    And dared to defy his rules.
But the stories of Kahless,
    Proud to be Klingon, and fierce,
    Intrigued Kortar despite his rage.
The people tell the tales with pride,
    And everywhere Kortar went,
    All proud warriors were gone.
Gone to do battle with Kahless,
    Kahless, Kahless, Kahless,
    All he heard was Kahless.
Still, Kortar cannot let a mortal
    Pass his gates and return alive,
    Kahless must be hunted down and killed.
Following the trail of Kahless,
    Kortar heads for the city of Qam-Chee,[*]
    Where he plans to kill this mortal.
Outside Qam-Chee,
    Kahless tells his warriors
    To go to the Saq'sub.

---

[*] Qam-Chee (*qamchIy*) is a Klingon city on Kronos. The Battle of Qam-Chee (*paq'raD* 13) took place at around 1373 CE; cf. MA, s.v. "Qam-Chee."

## 9. pong ghoj qortar

Daq HopHa'Daq                                            1
   qa'chaj nejlI'
   qortar qempa'QeH je
Dung qo' lupawDI' chaH
   qeylIS qorDu'Daj je ta''e' neH          5
   bop bommey
veqlarghvo' narghbogh loD
   chutDaj bIv 'e' ngIlbogh loD
   DaH pongDaj Sov qortar
QeHqu' qortar 'ach luvuQ                                 10
   tlhIngan ghaHmo' 'ej qu'mo'
   qeylIS Hem Delbogh lutmeyvam'e'
lut ja'taHvIS Hem rewbe'
   'ej Dat SuchDI' qortar
   Dach Hoch SuvwI'pu' Hem                   15
ghobmeH qeylIS lutlhej
   qeylIS qeylIS qeylIS
   qeylIS bop Hoch'e' Qoybogh qortar
lojmItDaj veghta'DI' jubbe'wI'
   yInqa'meH chegh 'e' botnIS qortar         20
   qeylIS HoHmeH qortar qeylIS SamnIS
qeylIS He tlha'meH
   qamchIy veng ghoSlI' qortar
   pa' jubbe'wI'vam HoH 'e' nab
qamchIy HurDaq                                           25
   SuvwI'pu'Daj ra' qeylIS
   SaqSub yIjaH

MOS  He will meet them there
(CONT.)   With the last of the warriors,
    He hopes to find around Qam-Chee.

pa' chaH ghomqa' ghaH     28
    qamchIyDaq SuvwI'pu' Qav tu' qeylIS 'e' tul
    'ej qeylIS lutlhej     30

## 10. The Feast at Qam-Chee

MOS  Upon entering the city,
      Kahless knows his tale
      Has preceded him.
  He is welcomed by Kahnrah,
      Patriarch of Qam-Chee,
      They have prepared a feast.

KAH  I thank you
      For the bloodwine and *gagh*,[*]
      We celebrate, for tomorrow we could die.

KNR  I thank you, for your stories of pride,
      Let me show you
      My two brave sons and my daughter.

KAH  I am honored to meet you,
      Sons of Kahnrah,
      And who is this?

LUK  My name is Lady Lukara, my friend,
      Your eyes show more bloodthirstiness
      Than I have ever seen!

KNR  Lukara! Leave him be,
      Can't you see he is tired?
      Kahless, my apologies.

---

[*] Gagh (*qagh*) is a Klingon delicacy made of serpent worms, preferrably consumed live. See also *paq'QIH* 4.18.

## 10. qamchIy 'uQ'a'

veng 'elDI' ghaH  1
    pawpa' ghaH'e'
    paw lutDaj 'e' Sov qeylIS
ghaH rI' 'ej quvmoH
    qanra' qamchIy qup'a'  5
    'uQ'a' luvutta'

'Iw HIq qagh je chojabpu'mo'
    qatlho'
    wa'leS chaq maHegh vaj malop

le'yo' lutmey juja'pu'mo' qatlho'  10
    cha' puqloDpu'wI' puqbe'wI' je
    qa'ang vIneH

batlh SaqIH
    qanra' puqloDpu'
    'ej 'Iv ghaH nuvvam'e'  15

luqara' 'oH pongwIj'e' jupwI'
    bIralqu' 'e' lu'ang mInDu'lIj
    SoH ral law'law' Hoch ral puSlaw'

luqara' yInuQQo'
    Doy' ghaH 'e' Datu'laHbe''a'  20
    qeylIS qatlhIjneS

KAH  The Lady Lukara is right, Kahnrah,
       I have shared stories of pride with you,
       Now I will tell you why I am here.
    Lukara, please sit by me,
       And listen to my tale,
       You look like you can help me.

lugh luqara' joH qanra'     22
  le'yo' lutmey Saja'pu'
  naDev vIpawta' 'ej DaH meqwIj Saja'
jIH retlhDaq yIba'neS     25
  'ej lutwIj yIQoy
  choQaHlaw'

### 11. Molor's Attack

MOS  Then Kahless tells his tale,
    The tale that inspired many before them,
    And every Klingon in the room falls silent.
Stories travel faster than a *khrun*,[*]
    Thus the stories of Kahless
    Also reach Molor's house.
Frightened by this revolution,
    Molor also decides to kill Kahless,
    Before the battle can start.
Molor sends five hundred
    Of his warriors to Qam-Chee
    To raid the town and kill Kahless.
So there they are,
    At Qam-Chee's gates,
    Demanding to get in.
In the name
    Of Molor the Mighty,
    Demanding to get in.
The men of Qam-Chee,
    They all back away
    From the gates and Molor's men.
Kahless climbs onto the table,
    Turns to the people,
    And spoke these words.

---

[*] A *khrun* (Hun) is an animal native to Kronos, used as a riding animal; cf. MB, s.v. "Khrun." As is suggested by the figure of speech in line 4, it is very fast.

## 11. HIv molor

ghIq lutDaj jatlh qeylIS                                      1
   latlhpu' law' pIlmoHpu' lutvam
   pa'Daq tamchoH Hoch tlhIngan
nom leng Hun nom lengqu' lut
   vaj molor juH lupaw je                         5
   qeylIS lutmey
ghaH ghIj Daw'vam
   lulchoHlaHpa' chaH
   qeylIS HoH 'e' wuq je molor
veng luweHmeH 'ej qeylIS luHoHmeH       10
   qamchIyDaq vagh vatlh SuvwI'pu'
   ngeH molor
vaj pa' SaH chaH
   qamchIy lojmItmeyDaq
   'el chaH 'e' luqap                              15
molor HoSghaj woQ
   luDoQ
   'el chaH 'e' lupoQ
lojmItvo' molor neghvo' je
   DoH                                              20
   qamchIy Hoch negh
raSDaq toS qeylIS
   rewbe'pu'Daq Qeq'egh
   'ej mu'meyvam jatlh

### 12. The Lady Lukara

KAH  Warriors of Qam-Chee,
    These are the men I tell you of,
    They have come for my blood.
Will you stand with me and defeat them?
    Will you?
    Will you?
Why are you all silent?
    You, proud warriors, are you afraid?
    And you, sons of Kahnrah, speak up!
Is there nobody in this hall
    Prepared to die for the honor
    Of your tribe and city?

LUK  People of Qam-Chee,
    The warrior before you
    Carries the essence of honor.
Yet you will not join your blades with his,
    I for one will stand with him
    To face the hordes outside.
And if I die,
    I do so next to a brave Klingon,
    I will at least die with honor!

MOS  The people of Qam-Chee,
    They fled their territory,
    And were killed one by one.
By the five hundred of Molor,
    By the five hundred of Molor,
    By the five hundred of Molor.

## 12. luqara' joH

qamchIy SuvwI'  1
   tlhIHvaD SuvwI'pu'vam vIDelpu'
   muHoHmeH pawpu'
DIjeymeH tutlhej'a'
   tutlhej'a'  5
   tutlhej'a'
qatlh Sutamchu' tlhIH
   SuvwI'pu' Hem boghIjlu''a'
   tlhIH je qanra' puqloD pejatlh
vaSvamDaq  10
   tuq veng je quvvaD
   Heghqangbogh SuvwI' tu'be'lu''a'

qamchIy rewbe'pu'
   batlhna' 'agh
   SuvwI' boleghbogh  15
'ach botlhejQo' SuSuvQo'
   vItlhejbej jIH
   Hur ghom'a' wIqaD
vaj jIHeghchugh
   tlhIngan yoH retlhDaq jIHegh  20
   'ej batlh jIHegh

yerchajvo' Haw'
   qamchIynganpu'
   ngIq nuv luHoH
molor vaghvatlh  25
   molor vaghvatlh
   molor vaghvatlh

### 13. The Battle of Qam-Chee

MOS   Kahless and Lukara,
      They fought in the Great Hall
      Against Molor's five hundred.
  Many hours of bloodshed passed,
      The Great Hall filled with the blood
      Of Molor's warriors.

ALL   So the bond was sealed in blood
      Of two equal in body and thought,
      The bond of life.

MOS   Fighting side by side
      Against the odds
      For survival together.
  Then Kahless's *bat'leth*
      Pierced the last of them.
      Showered with the soldiers' blood,
  They mated,
      They mated,
      They mated.

ALL   So the bond was sealed in blood
      Of two equal in body and thought,
      The bond of life.
  The band of warriors then went
      Past the shore to the river Skral,
      To Molor's seat of power.
  One by one Molor's scouts return,
      He asks them which banner
      Kahless marches under.

## 13. qamchIy may'

vaS'a'vetlhDaq 1
   molor vaghvatlh
   lul qeylIS luqara' je
qaStaHvIS rep law' Hargh
   vaS'a' teb 5
   molor SuvwI'pu' 'Iw

vaj ruS cher 'Iw
   rap cha' ghot HoS rap cha' ghot vuD
   chen yIn ruS

nItebHa' yIntaHmeH 10
   Sanchaj luqaD
   nItebHa' SuvlI'
ghIq QavwI'chaj DuQchu'
   qeylIS betleH
   chaH vel negh 'Iw ghaylu'pu'mo' 15
nga'chuq
   nga'chuq
   nga'chuq

vaj ruS cher 'Iw
   rap cha' ghot HoS rap cha' ghot vuD 20
   chen yIn ruS
ghIq SIqralDaq
   molor HoS waw' lupawmeH
   bIQtIq HeH juS SuvwI' ghom
nIteb chegh molor ngIq ghoqwI' 25
   joqwI''e' cha'bogh qeylIS
   luDel 'e' ra' molor

MOS   They reply it is the *meQboghnom*,\*
(CONT.)       The banner of unity
        And revolution.
    Molor asks them
        What weapons this army carries,
        They reply, shaped as the crescent moon.†

ALL   So the bond was sealed in blood
        Of two equal in body and thought,
        The bond of life.

---

\* Kahless's *meQboghnom* banner, a name composed from the roots "burn" (*meQ*), "to be born" (*bogh*), and "fast" (*nom*), expresses his revolutionary intentions.

† The weapons shaped as the crescent moon (*maS'e' loQ So'be'bogh QIb*) are obviously the *bat'leths* wielded by Kahless and his allies.

lujang meQboghnom 'oH 28
    yeqchu'taHghach Daw' je
    'oS joqwI' 30
nuH'e' qengbogh mangghomvam
    Del 'e' ra' molor
    lujang maS'e' loQ So'be'bogh QIb lurur

vaj ruS cher 'Iw
    rap cha' ghot HoS rap cha' ghot vuD 35
    chen yIn ruS

### 14. Assembly at the River Skral

MOS After having sealed this bond in blood,
    The two lovers left for the river Skral,
    Where the assembled warriors awaited them.
Molor asks them,
    Who leads these armies,
    And they reply:
"Three men lead the army
    With one who is most impressive
    With a five pointed blade."
Molor is amused,
    He climbs a watch tower
    To see this Kahless.
At the same time
    Kortar and the Qempa'keh arrive
    At the camp.
First, Molor taunts Kahless,
    Then Kortar comes to Kahless's tent,
    And grabs Kahless by the neck.
This is what Kortar and Molor
    Have said to Kahless
    In the hours before battle.

## 14. SIqral bIQtIqDaq ghom

ruS cherDI' 'Iw                                      1
    SIqral bIQtIq lughoS cha' parmaqqay
    pa' ghomta' SuvwI' 'ej pa' loS chaH
mangghomvam DevwI'
    luDel 'e' ra' molor                              5
    vaj ghaH lujang
mangghom luDev wej loD
    wa' Doj law' Hoch Doj puS
    'etlhDaj jeq vagh DuQwI'Hom
molor vuQlu'                                         10
    tu'taHmeH chalqach toS
    qeylISvam legh neHmo'
quqtaHvIS wanI'vam
    raQDaq pawta'
    qortar qempa'QeH je                              15
bI'reS qeylIS vaq molor
    ghIq qeylIS jo'ley' ghoS qortar
    'ej qeylIS mong 'uchchoH
may' lunungbogh repmey'e'
    qeylISvaD mu'meyvam                              20
    ja'ta' molor qortar je

### 15. Molor's Taunt

MOL Kahless, Kahless, Kahless,
>    You are but a glob fly!*
>    You sound irritating, but you lack the sting!
> Look at these *p'takhs* at your side,
>    They don't know how to distinguish
>    A sword from a plough!
> I will let my soldiers feast,
>    Give them blood wine
>    Until they can stand no more!
> Then, the morning after,
>    The battle will not be as short,
>    As it would be if my warriors were fit!
> Kahless, Kahless, Kahless,
>    I will finish what I have started!
>    You will die well!

---

\* Glob flies (*ghIlab ghew*) are insects indigenous to Kronos, about half the size of a Terran mosquito, who do not sting but produce a rather annoying sound, as Molor reminds us; cf. MA, s.v. "glob fly."

## 15. vaq molor

qeylIS qeylIS qeylIS  1
   ghIlab ghew neH SoH
   nuQ wablIj 'ach bI'aw'laHbe'
nItlhejbogh petaQmey
   tInuD chaHvaD  5
   nIb yan wIjwI' jan je
'uQ'a' Sop neghwI' 'e' vIchaw'
   ghaHvaD 'Iw HIq vInob
   ghIq SIbI'Ha' QamlaHbe'
ghIq po veb  10
   may' ngajHa'moH
   SuvwI'wI' ghobrupchu'be'ghach
qeylIS qeylIS qeylIS
   wanI' vItaghbogh vIrInmoH
   bIHeghqu'  15

## 16. Kortar's Deal

KOR Give me three good reasons
    Not to squeeze this hand tight
    And kill you where you stand!

KAH The reason of my betrayal
    Was my family honor,
    I want to restore this honor.
With it, I restore pride and values
    Of the Klingon Empire, for under Molor,
    They have grown weak and faint.

KOR You may go on as planned
    And confront Molor,
    My Qempa'keh will be at your side.
In return, you must go back
    With your brother and father
    To the Underworld.
You will join me afterward
    In the realm of the dead,
    Where you should have been right now.

KAH I will accept your proposal,
    But only if you grant me
    One condition:
I will restore honor among the living,
    You will restore honor
    Among the dead.
The honorable will be rewarded
    After death chooses to bring them to you,
    If you make it so, I accept.

## 16. lay' qortar

wejlogh choponlaHbe'chugh  1
   vaj ghopvam vItap
   'ej DaH naDev qaHoH

qorDu'wIj quvmo' jImaghpu'
   qorDu'wIj quvqa'moHlu'meH  5
   jIvang vIneH
tlhIngan wo' nur ghob je
   HoSmoH quvvam
   che'DI' molor nur ghob je pujchoHpu'

nablIj yIpab  10
   molor yIqaD
   nItlhej qempa'QeHwI'
bImej 'e' vIchaw'mo'
   ghe'tor cheghDI' loDnI'lI' vavlI' je
   chaH DatlhejnIS  15
ghIq Heghpu'wI'pu' qo'Daq
   jIH chomuv SoH
   Daqna'lIj 'oH

ghu' Dachupbogh vIlaj
   'ach wa' ghu' vIchupbogh  20
   Dalajchugh neH
yIntaHwI'pu' vImIlHa'moH jIH
   Heghpu'wI'pu'
   DamIlHa'moH SoH
SoHvaD quvwI' qem Hegh 'e' wIvDI' Hegh  25
   pop Hevchugh quvwI'
   'ej 'e' DaqaSmoHchugh jIlaj

### 17. The Battle at the River Skral

MOS   Kortar thinks about this for a while,
      Then without a word,
      He releases Kahless and walks away.
  The three forks of the Skral
      Were the scene of battle
      Between the two armies.
  Many of the warriors fell,
      The river ran red with the blood
      Of a glorious battle!

ALL   One by one they fell,
      Hearts were pierced,
      Heads were severed.

MOS   The lethal *bat'leths*
      Ripped open armor,
      And cut off legs in a single stroke.
  First, Morath fell,
      Fighting three men at once,
      A fatal wound in his neck killed him.
  Then, Kanjit fell,
      Fighting at Kahless's side,
      Killing one enemy while he fell.

ALL   One by one they fell,
      Hearts were pierced,
      Heads were severed.

## 17. SIqral bIQtIq may'

ghu'vam qellI' qortar　　　　　　　　　　　　1
　　ghIq pagh jatlhtaHvIS
　　qeylIS 'uchHa' 'ej ghaHvo' yIt
SIqral wej bIQtIqHommeyDaq
　　　Hargh　　　　　　　　　　　　　　　5
　　cha' mangghom
Hegh SuvwI'pu' law'
　　may'mo'
　　bIQtIq teb 'Iw Doq

Hegh wa' ghIq Hegh latlh　　　　　　　　　10
　　tIqDu' luDuQlu'
　　nachDu' luteqlu'

yoDmey pe'ta' betleHmey Qob
　　wa'logh mup betleH
　　'ej 'uSDu' teqta'　　　　　　　　　　　15
wa'DIch Hegh moratlh
　　wej SuvwI' SuvtaHvIS
　　mongDaj DuQlu' 'ej Hegh
ghIq Hegh qanjIt
　　qeylIS retlhDaq Suv　　　　　　　　　20
　　wa' jagh HoHta' HeghtaHvIS

Hegh wa' ghIq Hegh latlh
　　tIqDu' luDuQlu'
　　nachDu' luteqlu'

MOS  Kahless saw his father go down,
  It filled him with pride,
  He stood on the battlefield and screamed:

ALL  Kortar, Kortar, Kortar,
  Your two warriors approach you,
  They are bound for the Underworld!
 I have kept my word of honor,
  And so should you,
  Let endless battle and honor await them!

MOS  The rest of the warriors stopped,
  They stood and listened,
  To hear the mighty howl.
 They too started to shout to the heavens
  For the passage of their comrades,
  Their howls made Kronos's soil tremble.

ALL  Kortar, Kortar, Kortar
  Your two warriors approach you,
  They are bound for the Underworld!
 I have kept my word of honor,
  And so should you,
  Let endless battle and honor await them!

pum vavDaj 'e' legh qeylIS	25
   HemmoH
   che'ronDaq Qam 'ej jach

qortar qortar qortar
   nIghoS cha' SuvwI'lI'
   ghe'tor luleng	30
jIlay'ta' 'ej batlh jIpabta'
   vaj choDanIS
   reH batlh SuvtaHjaj chaH

vIHbe'choH latlh SuvwI'pu'
   bey HoS QoymeH	35
   'IjmeH QamtaH
juSmeH qochpu'chaj
   jachtaHvIS je chal luSIch beychaj
   'ej Qo'noS yav luQommoH

qortar qortar qortar	40
   nIghoS cha' SuvwI'lI'
   ghe'tor luleng
jIlay'ta' 'ej batlh jIpabta'
   vaj choDanIS
   reH batlh SuvtaHjaj chaH	45

## 18. The Tower of Molor

MOS  Many brave warriors fall
    By the hand of Kahless,
    In his path to Molor.
Molor,
    He does not do battle,
    From his tower, he watches his troops
First, he watches the battle smiling,
    Then, he sees many of his troops fall,
    Then, he sees the Qempa'keh,
These fearsome warriors,
    They fight without remorse,
    And there is fire in their eyes.
Now Kahless and the Qempa'keh,
    They reach the base
    Of Molor's guarded tower.
Kahless looks up and
    For the first time the two
    Meet eye to eye, and Kahless shouts.

## 18. molor chalqach

molorDaq He ghoStaHvIS     1
   yoHbogh SuvwI' law'
   pummoH qeylIS ghop
molor
   ghobbe'     5
   chalqachDajvo' QaSDaj bej
may' bI'reS bejtaHvIS mon
   ghIq pum QaSDaj law' 'e' legh
   ghIq qempa'QeH legh
SuvwI'pu'vam qu'     10
   not may' lupay chaH
   'ej qul lungaS mInDu'chaj
DaH molor chalqach 'avlu'bogh
   qappam lupawta'
   qeylIS qempa'QeH je     15
yor lunej qeylIS mIn 'ej
   qIHchuq cha' loD mIn
   'ej jach qeylIS

### 19. Molor Taunts Kahless

KAH  Traitor of Kronos,
    Traitor of the Saq'sub,
    Traitor of our race!
Come down from your tower,
    And fight me ridge to ridge,
    And blade to blade!

MOL  Be gone with you, Kahless,
    Warrior of the slaves,
    Leader of evil spirits!
You dirty *p'takh*,
    Your word means nothing to me,
    Don't speak to me of honor!
Did you think that my word of honor
    Would have carried me this far?
    Honor is for those with nothing to lose!

## 19. qeylIS vaq molor

Qo'noS 'urwI'  1
  SaqSub 'urwI'
  Seghmaj 'urwI'
chalqachlIjvo' yIghIr
  QuchwIj vIl Suvjaj QuchlIj vIl  5
  'etlhwIj Suvjaj 'etlhlIj

yImej qeylIS
  toy'wI''a' SuvwI'
  qa'pu' mIgh DevwI'
petaQ'a' SoH  10
  bIlay'DI' qaHarbe'
  jIHvaD quv yIjatlhQo'
jIlay'mo' 'ej batlh jIpabmo'
  Qapla' vIchavta' 'e' DaHar'a'
  quv vuv nuv pagh ghajchugh neH  15

## 20. The Mighty Blow of the *Bat'leth*

ALL   Molor, Molor, Molor,
      You cannot escape your fate,
      Even in a tower you are not safe!

MOS   You have awoken Kahless's anger,
      His muscles filled with rage,
      His mind focused and clear.
The *bat'leth* sunk into the post
      Of your fortified tower,
      All his rage focussed in one blow

ALL   Molor, Molor, Molor,
      You cannot escape your fate,
      Even in a tower you are not safe!

MOS   You stood there, you attack
      Like a *krencha*,[*] short and fierce,
      Avoiding long and dangerous battle.
But now your tower rumbles,
      And soon it will disappear
      From under your feet.

ALL   Molor, Molor, Molor,
      You cannot escape your fate,
      Even in a tower you are not safe!

---

[*] A *krencha* (*QIncha'*) is a type of lizard indigenous to Kronos.

## 20. pe'vIl mupmeH betleH Qach

molor molor molor  1
   SanIIj DanarghlaHbe'
   chalqachDaq bIQaDbe'\*\* je

qeylIS QeH DavemmoHpu'
   SomrawDu'Daj teb qajunpaQ  5
   qImchoHlaHchu' yabDaj
chalqachlIj rachlu'ta'bogh tutDaq
   mol'egh betleH
   muptaHvIS tay''eghmoH QeHDaj Hoch

molor molor molor  10
   SanIIj DanarghlaHbe'
   chalqachDaq bIQaDbe' je

pa' bIQam bIHIvDI'
   QIncha' Darur qu' 'ej run
   Qobbogh may' nI' jun  15
'ach DaH Qom chalqachlIj
   'ej qamDu'lIj bIngvo'
   tugh ngabchu' 'oH

molor molor molor
   SanIIj DanarghlaHbe'  20
   chalqachDaq bIQaDbe' je

---

\* See *paq'raD* 1, note ad loc.

MOS  Now the mighty structure
        Comes down to the ground,
        Together with your pride.
     Kahless grips you by the throat,
        He could rip your hearts out at will,
        But instead he put you on your feet.

ALL  Molor, Molor, Molor,
        You cannot escape your fate,
        Even in a tower you are not safe!

DaH yavDaq Dej 22
   qach rachlu'ta'bogh
   tlhej le'yo'lIj
HughlIj 'uch qeylIS 25
   DaH rolIjvo' tIqDu'lIj lellaH
   'ach DuQammoH

molor molor molor
   SanlIj DanarghlaHbe'
   chalqachDaq bIQaDbe' je 30

### 21. The Challenge

KAH  Look me in the eye, Molor,
    I gave you my word of honor,
    And I will respect it.
I have let you out of your tower alive,
    Now prepare for battle to the death,
    Sharpen your blade, meet me tomorrow.
Sleep well, for it will be your last night,
    Put on your finest armor,
    For there is no honor in attacking the weak.
I will show you strength,
    I will show you blood,
    I will show you honor!

## 21. qaD

mInDu'wIj tIbuS molor 1
   SoHvaD jIlay'ta'
  'ej batlh jIpab
chalqachlIj Damejpu' 'ej bIyIn 'e' vIchaw'
   DaH yISuvrupchu' 5
  'etlhlIj yIjejmoH wa'leS HIghom
ramvam yIQongqu' ram veb bIyInbe'
   may'luchlIj nIv yItuQmoH
  pujwI' HIvlu'chugh quvbe'lu'
SoHvaD HoS vI'agh 10
   SoHvaD 'Iw vI'agh
   SoHvaD quv vI'agh

## 22. The Opponents Meet

MOS  Kahless slaps Molor
     With the back of his hand,
     And walks away.

ALL  The sun rises high behind the Kri'stak,
     When it rises over its top,
     It is time to do battle.

MOS  There they stand, two mortal enemies,
     Ready to fight to the death
     In hand to hand combat.
  Their armies stand and watch,
     Unarmed, at a distance,
     The war will be decided by two.

ALL  The sun rises high behind the Kri'stak,
     When it rises over its top,
     It is time to do battle.

## 22. ghom gholpu'

molor qIpmeH                                            1
   wa' chap lo' qeylIS
   'ej ghaHvo' yIt

QIStaq 'emDaq jenchoH jul
   yor DungDaq Salta'DI'                  5
   tagh HarghchuqmeH poH

pa' Qam cha' jaghpu' naS
   Suvchuqrupchu'
   cholchuq chaH
Qam mangghomchaj 'ej bej                                10
   nuHmey lonta' 'ej Hop
   noHvam charghwI'pu' wuq cha' SuvwI'

QIStaq 'emDaq jenchoH jul
   yor DungDaq Salta'DI'
   tagh HarghchuqmeH poH                  15

### 23. The Duel

ALL   Kahless and Molor,
      The strength of your hearts
      Will decide what is to come.
  And they battle, for three hours,
      Kahless's *bat'leth* sparks,
      And Molor's mighty sword roars.

MOS   Both Klingon hearts beat,
      At their strongest,
      In lust for blood.
  In the first hour,
      Kahless cut off Molor's beard,
      Molor fought harder, fierce and ashamed.

ALL   Kahless and Molor,
      The strength of your hearts
      Will decide what is to come.
  And they battle, for three hours,
      Kahless's *bat'leth* sparks,
      And Molor's mighty sword roars.

MOS   Both bodies grew tired,
      And felt the pain,
      But their hearts knew only bloodthirstiness.
  In the second hour,
      Kahless broke Molor's sword in half,
      Shame turned to fear in Molor's eyes.

## 23. Hay' chaH

qeylIS molor je                                          1
   Sanmaj chenmoH
   tIqDu'raj HoS
qaStaHvIS wej rep
     pan qeylIS betleH                              5
   'ej jach molor 'etlh HoS

Hay'chu' luneHqu'
   vaj pe'vIl joqqu'
   cha' tlhIngan tIqDu'
qaStaHvIS rep wa'DIch                                    10
   molor rol chIpchu' qeylIS 'ej teq
   tuH molor 'ach ghur QeH 'ej pe'vIl HarghlI'

qeylIS molor je
   Sanmaj chenmoH
   tIqDu'raj HoS                                     15
qaStaHvIS wej rep
   pan qeylIS betleH
   'ej jach molor 'etlh HoS

Doy'choH cha' porgh
   'oy' cha' porgh                                   20
   'ach Hay'chu' luneH neH tIqDu'chaj
qaStaHvIS rep cha'DIch
   molor 'etlh bID wItlh qeylIS
   tuH 'e' mev 'ej ghIjlu' 'e' lu'ang molor mInDu'

MOS   Kahless and Molor,
       The strength of your hearts
         Will decide what is to come.
     And they battle, for three hours,
       Kahless's *bat'leth* sparks,
       And Molor's mighty sword roars.

ALL   It was not long, by the third hour,
       Before Kahless struck his *bat'leth*
         Right into Molor's hearts, ripping them out.
     In one single move, he removed the hearts,
       In one single move, he restored his honor,
       In one single move, the battle was done.

MOS   Kahless and Molor,
       The strength of your hearts
         Will decide what is to come.
     And they battle, for three hours,
       Kahless's *bat'leth* sparks,
       And Molor's mighty sword roars.

ALL   In one single move,
       Kahless decided the fate
         Of thousands, and those to come.
     Kahless takes Molor's hearts,
       Still beating, to the river Skral,
       He sets them free in the crimson water.

qeylIS molor je 25
   Sanmaj chenmoH
   tIqDu'raj HoS
qaStaHvIS wej rep
   pan qeylIS betleH
   'ej jach molor 'etlh HoS 30

tugh qaStaHvIS rep wejDIch
   molor cha' tIqDu' DuQchu' qeylIS
   'ej lel
ngIq tonSaw' lo' 'ej tIqDu' lel
   ngIq tonSaw' lo' 'ej quvqa'moH 35
   ngIq tonSaw' lo' 'ej rIn may'

qeylIS molor je
   Sanmaj chenmoH
   tIqDu'raj HoS
qaStaHvIS wej rep 40
   pan qeylIS betleH
   'ej jach molor 'etlh HoS

ngIq tonSaw' lo'
   SaD law' San chenmoH qeylIS
   wej boghbogh nuvpu' San chenmoH 45
SIqral bIQtIqDaq
   joqtaHbogh molor tIqDu' qem qeylIS
   bIQ DoqDaq tlhabmoH*

---

\*   The last lines of canto 23 also appear in a Klingon drinking song, attested in : "And the River Skral ran crimson red" (*'ej Doq SoDtaH ghoSpa' S[I]qral bIQtIq*) cf. DS9:4x01; MA, s.v. "Klingon drinking songs."

### 24. Molor's Release[*]

KAH  May these waters wash clean
    These hearts,
    Blackened with shame.
So that one day Molor will see
    The folly of his treacherous ways,
    And embrace the ways of honor.
May Kortar be merciful on his spirit,
    For no matter his faults, at least
    This Klingon brother died with honor.

---

[*] The meaning of "release" (*tlhabmoH,* lit. "cause to be free") here is a matter of dispute among Klingon scholars. It may refer to Molor's release from the life on Kronos to the afterlife, or more specifically to the release from the burden of dishonor in the land of the living. The precise relation between transition to the afterlife and Klingon honor was an object of heavy debate among the different Klingon sects that developed in the wake of Kahless's death.

## 24. molor tlhabmoHlu'

tIqDu'vam tuHqu'  1
   Say'moHchu'jaj
   bIQtIqvam
matlhHa'lu'chugh vaj Doghlu'
   'e' yajmeH molor  5
   'ej batlh vangchoHmeH molor
qa'Daj vupjaj qortar
   puj ghaH
   'ach batlh Heghpu' tlhInganvam

paq'raD

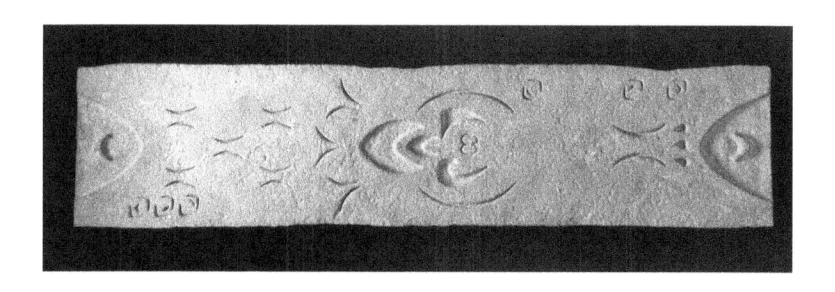

*Figs.* 3a–c: TL–C, the musical score for the love making scene between Kahless and Lady Lukara in *paq'raD* 13, "The Battle of Qam-Chee" (*qamchIy may'*).

Impact Book

paq'QIH

## 1. Kahless Departs

ALL   Oh,
>Kahless, Kahless, Kahless,
>Son of Kanjit,

>Klingon Father,
>>Wise and brave,
>>You have succeeded.

MOS   And so Kahless slew the tyrant Molor,
>>And taught the people the ways of honor
>>By his words and his honorable deeds.

>Kahless united the tribes of Kronos,
>>And provided them with the laws of honor,
>>He was crowned Emperor of the Klingon Empire.

ALL   Oh,
>Kahless, Kahless, Kahless,
>Son of Kanjit,

>Klingon Father,
>>Wise and brave,
>>You have succeeded.

MOS   The Klingon tribes flourished once more,
>>And many great victories were made
>>During Kahless's reign of wisdom and bravery.

>Then, the time came when Kahless saw
>>That his work on Kronos was done,
>>He did not forget Kortar.

## 1. tlheD qeylIS

'o
   qeylIS qeylIS qeylIS
   qanjIt puqloD
tlhIngan vav
   bIchul 'ej bIyoH
   bIQapta'

vaj molor HoHta' qeylIS
   'ej quv tIghmey
   'aghpu' mu'meyDaj ta'meyDaj je
Qo'noS tuqmey muvchuqmoH qeylIS
   'ej chaHvaD batlh chutmey nob
   tlhIngan wo' voDleH moj Sughlu'

'o
   qeylIS qeylIS qeylIS
   qanjIt puqloD
tlhIngan vav
   bIchul 'ej bIyoH
   bIQapta'

che'taHvIS chul qeylIS 'ej yoH
   Qapqa' tlhIngan tuqmey
   'ej yaymey Dun chav
ghIq Qo'noSDaq Qap rIntaH 'e' Sov
   qeylIS
   qortar lIjbe'

ALL  Oh,
    Kahless, Kahless, Kahless,
    Son of Kanjit,
Klingon Father,
    Wise and brave,
    You have succeeded.

MOS  On the night of the new moon
    Kahless gathered his weapons,
    And his finest suit of armor.
Thousands followed him
    To the edge of the city,
    To bid him farewell.

ALL  Oh,
    Kahless, Kahless, Kahless,
    Son of Kanjit,
Klingon Father,
    Wise and brave,
    You have succeeded.

'o
   qeylIS qeylIS qeylIS
   qanjIt puqloD
tlhIngan vav
   bIchul 'ej bIyoH
   bIQapta'

qaStaHvIS ram, maS So'lu'chu'DI'
   nuHmeyDaj may'luchDaj nIv je
   yIr qeylIS
tlheDDI' quvmoHmeH
   veng HeHDaq lutlha'
   SaD law' nuvpu'

'o
   qeylIS qeylIS qeylIS
   qanjIt puqloD
tlhIngan vav
   bIchul 'ej bIyoH
   bIQapta'

## 2. Kahless's Last Words

KAH  Remember forever that you are Klingons,
    You need no one but yourselves!
    I will go and join Kortar, to be with my kin.
Follow the honor in your spirit,
    And if you should loose your way,
    Remember the young warrior from the Saq'sub.
May you remember his deeds with pride,
    May you recite his words with wisdom,
    May they forever be unforgettable.

## 2. qeylIS mu'mey Qav

reH tlhIngan tlhIH 'e' yIqaw  1
   pewuv'egh
   qortar vImuv pal'arpu'wI' vImuv
qa'lI' quv yIpab
   'ej tIghmeylIj bolIjchugh  5
   SaqSub SuvwI' Qup yIqaw
ta'meyDaj boqawDI' SuHemjaj
   mu'meyDaj bojatlhDI' Suchuljaj
   not ta'meyDaj mu'meyDaj joq bolIjjaj

### 3. The *Hegh'bat*\* of Kahless

MOS These were the last words
    Of Kahless the unforgettable,
    Before Kortar's barge sailed in.
Kahless kept his word of honor to Kortar,
    After his last words, all were sent away,
    But his wife Lukara.
Lukara, pregnant of their first-born son,
    Understood what had to be done,
    And gave him the *mevak*.
Lady Lukara and Kahless,
    They said their goodbyes,
    And Lukara knew they would meet again.
Fighting side by side
    In an underworld, more glorious
    Than Gre'thor ever was.
Now, the time had come,
    Kahless impaled his hearts
    With the two blades of the *mevak*.
One blade to extinguish the physical life,
    One blade for freeing the soul,
    The Klingon's transition was complete.

---

\* A *hegh'bat* (Heghbat) is a ritual suicide comparable to the Japanese tradition of *seppuku*. The term supposedly consists of the roots "to die" (*Hegh*) and "honor" (*batlh*), their composition however would be ungrammatical in modern Klingon. In this scene Lady Lukara assists him by handing him a traditional *mevak* (*ma'veq*) knife to plunge into his hearts. As tradition dictates, she then takes the knife from him and wipes it on the sleeve of her dress. See MA, s.v. "hegh'bat."

## 3. qeylIS Heghbat

mu'meyvam Qav jatlh                                               1
  qeylIS lIjlaHbogh pagh*
  pawpa' qortar bIQ Duj
qortarvaD lay'ta' 'ej batlh pabta' qeylIS
  jatlh 'e' mevDI' nuvpu' mejmoH ghaH              5
  ratlh be'nalDaj luqara' neH
yatlh luqara' puqloD wa'DIch qenglI'
  Qu'Daj yajchu' ghaH
  qeylISvaD ma'veq nob
vanchuq luqara' joH qeylIS je                                 10
  'ej Hemey pIm ghoS
  qa' qo'Daq ghomqa' chaH
'ej nItebHa' Suv chaH
  'e' Sov luqara'
  qa' qo'vam Dun law' ghe'tor Dun puS         15
DaH wanI' potlh taghlu'
  tIqDu'Daj DuQqu'meH qeylIS
  ma'veq cha' 'etlhmey jop
porgh HoH wa' 'etlh
  qa' tlhabmoH wa' 'etlh                                20
  tlhIngan choHlu' rIntaH

---

\*  Line 2 of canto 3 features the first literal occurrence of Kahless's now classical epithet "The Unforgettable" (*qeylIS lIjlaHbogh pagh*).

MOS (CONT.)
Lukara wiped the blood on her sleeve,
    And cried out to Kortar to announce his arrival
        In the realm of the dead.
Kortar, Kortar, Kortar,
    Your warrior approaches you,
        He is bound for the Underworld!
I have kept my word of honor,
    And so should you,
        Let endless battle and honor await him!
All of Kronos trembled once more,
    For every Klingon on the planet
        Followed her cry for Kahless.
And so Kahless the unforgettable
    Returned to Gre'thor,
        To meet proud warriors at its gates.

'Iw teqmeH tlhayDaj lo' luqara'  22
   'ej qa' qo'Daq paw qeylIS 'e' maqmeH
   qortarvaD jach
qortar qortar qortar  25
   DughoS SuvwI'lI'
   ghe'tor leng
jIlay'ta' 'ej batlh jIpabta'
   vaj choDanIS
   reH batlh SuvtaHjaj ghaH  30
qeylISvaD jach 'ej beyDaj luqImmo'
   yuQDaq ghaHtaHbogh Hoch tlhIngan'e'
   Qomqa' Hoch Qo'noS nuvpu'
lojmItDaq SuvwI'pu' Hem qIHmeH
   qeylIS lIjlaHbogh pagh  35
   ghe'tor chegh

### 4. Kortar Creates Sto-vo-kor

MOS When the Barge of the Dead came,
    Kortar stood at its helm,
    Kanjit and Morath by his side.
The three were reunited once more,
    They set sail over the Blood River
    To Gre'thor, or so Kahless thought.
Not only Kahless remembered his words,
    Kortar also met his part
    Of the arrangement at Qam-Chee.
The barge entered a new underworld,
    Kortar named it Sto-vo-kor,
    Kahless looked at it with great pride.
Sto-vo-kor, a mighty stone castle,
    Where warriors returned after battle,
    To drink, eat, and celebrate.
Its towers grand, the space infinite,
    The smell of bloodwine and *gagh*
    Filled the barge upon entering.
At the centre of Sto-vo-kor,
    The ancient hearts of honor and wisdom
    Beat steady and strong.
Gre'thor was now the home
    Of the hearts of doubt and fear,
    The place for the weak and dishonored.
Kortar and Fek'lhr cooled their rage there,
    Slaying spirits with no honor,
    No honor, no hope, no future.
The barge went through Gre'thor
    Into the gates of Sto-vo-kor,
    Kahless was given a hero's welcome.

## 4. Suto'vo'qor chenmoH qortar

pawDI' Hegh Duj                                                   1
  DeghDaq Qam qortar
  qortar retlhDaq Qam qanjIt moratlh je
muvchuqqa' vav puqloDpu' je
  'Iw bIQtIqDaq ghe'tor leng                                      5
  'e' Har qeylIS
mu'meyDaj qawta' qeylIS
  'ach qamchIyDaq lay'ta' qortar
  'ej pabta' je
qa' qo' chu' 'el Duj                                              10
  'oHvaD Suto'vo'qor pong qortar
  'oH nuD qeylIS 'ej Hem
nagh jem'IH rachlu'ta'bogh 'oH Suto'vo'qor'e'
  Suv 'e' mevDI' tlhutlhmeH SopmeH lopmeH
  pa' chegh SuvwI'pu'                                             15
Doj chalqachDaj veHmey Hutlh
  pa' 'elDI' Duj
  'Iw HIq pIw qagh pIw je lularghlu'chu'
Suto'vo'qor botlhDaq
  pe'vIl joqchu'taH                                               20
  quvbogh 'ej chulbogh tIqDu' tIQ
Honbogh nuch tIqDu'vaD
  juH moj ghe'tor
  pujwI'vaD nuv quvHa'vaD je Daq moj
pa' QeHHa'choH qortar veqlargh je                                 25
  quv Hutlhbogh qa' HoH
  quv Hutlh ngoQ Hutlh San Hutlh
ghe'tor vegh Duj
  Suto'vo'qor lojmItmey 'el Duj
  qeylIS vanlu'chu' 'ej naDlu'chu'                                30

MOS (CONT.)
There was a feast with his kin,
    And the warriors that took part
    In the great battle against Molor.
After the feast, Kahless felt tired,
    He looked back on his words and deeds,
    And then slept for three days.
Kahless awoke from his sleep
    By the voice of Kortar
    Calling him to his feet.

'uQ'a' lutIv 31
   molor luHarghbogh SuvwI'pu'
   qeylIS pal'arpu'Daj je
rInDI' 'uQ'a' Doy' qeylIS
   mu'meyDaj ta'meyDaj je qaw 35
   'ej qaStaHvIS wej jaj Qong
qeylIS vemmoH
   qortar ghogh
   qIm neH

### 5. Kortar Gives Sto-vo-kor to Kahless

KOR Kahless the unforgettable,
    I welcome you in Sto-vo-kor,
    For you lived wise and honorable.
As you see, I have kept my word,
    I have built our proud warriors,
    A home in the afterlife.
The castle is perfect, although
    It has but one flaw,
    We need a trustworthy guard.
Since you are the only one
    Who ever entered Gre'thor,
    And left from its gates unharmed,
You are my best warrior,
    Therefore, you will guard
    The gate of Sto-vo-kor.
You will not only keep poor souls
    From entering the realm of the proud,
    You will also welcome the honorable.
You will offer them a place
    Between these walls,
    And a feast to their liking.
The Klingons with fear in their hearts
    And water in their veins
    Will stay in Gre'thor with me and Fek'lhr,
They will pay for the anger
    You caused by entering and leaving
    Gre'thor in search of your kin.

## 5. qeylISvaD Suto'vo'qor nob qortar

qeylIS lIjlaHbogh pagh 1
   Suto'vo'qorDaq qavan
   bIyIntaHvIS bIchul 'e' Da'agh 'ej batlh bIvang
bIleghlaH jIlay'ta' 'ej batlh jIpabta'
   qa' qo'Daq SuvwI'pu'ma' HemvaD 5
   juH vIchenmoH
pup jem'IH
   'ach wa' Duy' tu'lu'
   'avwI' wIvoqlaHbogh wIpoQ
ghe'tor Da'elta' 10
   'ej lojmItDajvo' Damejta'
   'ach bIrIQbe'mo' SoH neH
vaj SuvwI'wI' nIv SoH
   vaj Suto'vo'qor lojmIt
   Da'av 15
qa' Hem qo'
   lu'el qa' QIv 'e' Dabot
   lu'el qa' quv 'e' Dachaw'
tlhoy'mey jojDaq
   chaHvaD Daq Danob 20
   'ej chaHvaD 'uQ'a' lutIvbogh Danob
yoHbe'chugh tlhIngan tIqDu'
   'ej bIQ lungaSchugh tlhIngan 'aDDu'
   ghe'torDaq mutlhej 'ej veqlargh lutlhej
pal'arpu'lI' DaSammeH 25
   ghe'tor Da'elmo' 'ej Damejmo'
   QeHchoH qa'pu' vaj lubIjlu'

# Epilogue

bertlham

MOS  And so, the two ways of afterlife
         Were created by Kortar,
         And so it is, up to this day.
     Now, by the deeds of Kahless,
         Every Klingon knows the ways of honor,
         And teaches their children by this tale.
     Live the Klingon way,
         History is written by the victors,
         Celebrate death, for it is honorable.
     We fight to enrich the spirit
         And to expand our realm,
         Listen to the voice of your blood.
     Honor is more important than life,
         May your enemies run with fear,
         For you are Klingon, we are Klingon.
     Remember and live with honor,
         Remember and die with honor,
         For who dies honorable, dies well!

vaj cha' qa' qo'mey
   chenmoHta' qortar
   'ej jajmeyvam taH ghu'vam
DaH vangta'mo' qeylIS
   quv tIghmey Sov Hoch tlhIngan
   'ej puqpu'DajvaD lutvam jatlhqa'
tlhIngan tIgh yIpab
   qun qon charghwI'pu''e'
   quvmo' Hegh Hegh yInaD
qa' wIje'meH maSuv
   qo'maj wISachmeH maSuv
   'IwlIj ghogh yIQoy
batlh potlh law' yIn potlh puS
   ghIj qet jaghmeyjaj
   tlhIngan SoH tlhIngan maH
yIqaw 'ej batlh yIyIn
   yIqaw 'ej batlh yIHegh
   batlh Heghlu'chugh Heghlu'chu'

# Bibliography

PRIMARY SOURCES

The following sources and additional literature have been used in the reconstruction of sv.

o: Libretto for the opera *'u'* written in modern Klingon, partially reconstructed with TL. Contains elements from *yav*, *raD*, *QIH* books, and the epilogue. Earliest version probably from around 817 QB. Mainly written in first-person perspective except for the *Qich'lut* parts, following a classical 3-6 line structure.
op: Version in *no' Hol* of what is considered to be the original prologue of the *paq'batlh*, currently stored in the archives of the Volkenkunde Museum in Leiden. It deals with the origin myth of the Klingons in three parts. Dating back to at least 500 QBN. Written in third-person perspective with classical 3-6 line structure.

SV: Standard Version of the *paq'batlh* located on a server of the University of Heidelberg. Main source of the reconstructions, complementing material of O and OP.

TL-A, TL-B, TL-C: Also known as the Kijkduin Stones. Three triangular stones bearing carvings containing *no' Hol* fragments and pictograms. Thought to be used as a musical score. Fragments of two scenes from *paq'raD* and the story "The Fool and the Wind." Thought to be from around 100-150 QB. Included as figures 1, 2, and 3.

### SECONDARY SOURCES

Friedman, Michael-Jan. *Kahless*. New York: Pocket Books, 1997.

Okrand, Marc. *Klingon for the Galactic Traveler*. New York: Pocket Books, 1997.

———. *The Klingon Dictionary*. New York: Pocket Books, 1992.

———. *The Klingon Way: A Warrior's Guide*. New York: Pocket Books, 1996.

Okrent, Arika. *In the Land of Invented Languages: Adventures in Linguistic Creativity, Madness, and Genius*. New York: Spiegel & Grau, 2009.

Shakespeare, William. *Hamlet, Prince of Denmark*. Restored by Nick Nicholas and Andrew Strader. New York: Pocket Books, 2000.

## OTHER SOURCES

MA, MB: *Memory Alpha* and *Beta,* online anthropological databases covering, inter alia, Klingon culture. https://memory-alpha.fandom.com/wiki/Portal:Main; https://memory-beta.fandom.com/wiki/Main_Page.

KECP: *Klingon Extended Corpus Project,* online database of Klingon terms and names. https://www.kli.org/activities/extended-corpus/.

*HolQeD*: Journal for Klingon linguistics and philology. https://www.kli.org/resources/holqed/.

*Hol 'ampaS*: Online Klingon Language Academy with grammar, forum, and lessons. https://hol.kag.org/.